Merchandise Licensing in the Television Industry

Broadcast & Cable Series
Series Editor: Donald V. West, Editor/Senior Vice-President,
Broadcasting & Cable

Global Television: How to Create Effective Television for the 1990s
Tony Verna

The Broadcast Century: A Biography of American Broadcasting
Robert L. Hilliard and Michael C. Keith

*Global Telecommunications: The Technology, Administration and
    Policies*
Raymond Akwule

Selling Radio Direct
Michael C. Keith

Electronic Media Ratings
Karen Buzzard

International Television Co-Production: From Access to Success
Carla Brooks Johnston

Practical Radio Promotions
Ted E. F. Roberts

The Remaking of Radio
Vincent M. Ditingo

The Global Television News Game
Carla Brooks Johnston

Merchandise Licensing in the Television Industry

by
Karen Raugust

Focal Press
Boston   Oxford   Melbourne   Singapore   Toronto
Munich   New Delhi   Tokyo

Focal Press is an imprint of Butterworth–Heinemann

Copyright © 1996 by Butterworth–Heinemann

Library of Congress Cataloging-in-Publication Data
Raugust, Karen, 1960–
    Merchandise licensing in the television industry / by Karen
Raugust.
        p.   cm. — (Broadcasting & cable series)
    Includes index.
    ISBN 0–240–80210–1
    1. Television broadcasting—Licenses—United States—History.
2. Cable television—Licenses—United States—History.
3. Merchandise licensing—United States—History.   4. License
agreements—United States—History.   I. Series.
HE8700.8.R38   1995
384.55′1—dc20   95–18998
                                                                              CIP

British Library Cataloguing-in-Publication Data
A catalogue record for this book is available from the British Library.

The publisher offers discounts on bulk orders of this book.
For information, please write:

Manager of Special Sales
Butterworth–Heinemann
313 Washington Street
Newton, MA 02158–1626

10 9 8 7 6 5 4 3 2 1

Printed in the United States of America

1

Table of Contents

Acknowledgments

Special thanks to all of the people who provided information for this book. In particular, the cooperation of Britt Allcroft, Inc., Hamilton Projects, Hanna-Barbera, Nickelodeon, Turner Licensing & Merchandising, and Viacom Consumer Products in providing specifics for the case studies is gratefully acknowledged. Thanks also to EPM Communications for allowing the use of various facts and figures from *The Licensing Letter*.

This book is dedicated to Michael Partney

Introduction

Merchandise licensing is big business. More than $66.5 billion worth of licensed products were sold at retail in 1993 in the United States and Canada alone, according to *The Licensing Letter*, an industry trade publication. Almost 24% of that, or nearly $16 billion, was attributable to television, film, and character licensing, a segment that grew 12% from 1992 to 1993.

In fact, licensed properties with origins in television have been among the most popular in recent years, with PBS shows alone—*Sesame Street*, *Shining Time Station*, *Barney & Friends*, and *Lamb Chop's Play-Along*, for example—responsible for an estimated $1.5 billion in retail sales in 1993. Those sales figures translate, conservatively, to about $56 million in royalties earned by the property owners. The hottest children's programs, such as *Teenage Mutant Ninja Turtles* or *Mighty Morphin Power Rangers*, surpass $1 billion in total retail sales of licensed merchandise.

Television licensing is not limited to children's properties, however. Live-action programs watched by adults, among them the *Star Trek* franchise and *Northern Exposure*, lend themselves to licensed products, from trading cards and action figures to stuffed toys and sweatshirts. Licensing efforts based on television brands, including ABC Sports and the Cartoon Network, can be lucrative as well.

There is little wonder, then, that more and more television executives are looking at merchandise licensing as a viable way to create additional profit centers. The major networks are exploring licensing more actively, as are independent syndicators and program producers, among them Lancit Media, Bohbot Entertainment, Film Roman, and ITC, all of which have set up in-house licensing staffs. More cable networks are also making forays into licensing, partly to create brand awareness and partly to capitalize on the characters starring in their original programming.

Merchandise Licensing in the Television Industry is written for those in the cable and broadcast television industries who need to know more about merchandise licensing. It is aimed at everyone from the executive whose company is exploring licensing for the first time, to new employees responsible for an existing licensing program. It is for anyone in the industry who has anything to do with licensing: legal counsel, marketing departments, consumer products divisions, licensing agents, and executive offices.

The book will provide a historical perspective of television licensing from the early days to the present. It will examine current and future trends and how they affect television-based merchandising. It will explain the nuts and bolts of how to set up a licensing program. And it will contain lots of examples, including a whole chapter of case studies, to illustrate the points made throughout the book.

It should be remembered that things change. Product lines, promotional plans, broadcast schedules, and numerical information alter on a daily basis. Licensing programs and television productions come and go. While every effort was made to ensure the accuracy of all the information in this book at the time of its writing, some of the specifics may become slightly dated over time. The ideas and trends, however, will still be relevant.

Despite the fact that licensing is big business, and of great significance to its practitioners, it can also be fun. After all, one can't be *too* serious when discussing *Biker Mice From Mars* balloons, *Care Bears* candy, or *Animaniacs* toys.

Karen Raugust
Brooklyn, NY

Chapter 1

Basics and Background

Television executives increasingly consider merchandise licensing a potentially significant marketing technique. As the terrestrial broadcast and cable industries witness more competition and as television programs become more costly to produce, licensing is perceived as an important method of creating awareness and generating revenues.

What Is Merchandise Licensing?

The following situation illustrates the essence of a licensing deal: the owner of a television series (or of the rights to merchandise it) grants a company permission to manufacture products incorporating the television program's name or logo, or to use artwork, characters, or other elements related to the show. In return for that permission, the owner receives payment, usually in the form of a royalty on each item sold.

A licensing contract is analogous to a rental agreement. The owner of the rights allows the manufacturer to use the television show for a finite time period, on certain products, within an agreed-upon geographic area, through a specified distribution network, all in return for payment. The licensable entity—whether a name, logo, character, or other component of the show—must first

1

be legally protected under trademark and/or copyright laws, and is known as the "property." The owner of the property is called the "licensor" and the manufacturer, the "licensee."

Benefits of licensing

For the licensor, merchandise licensing can be beneficial in two major ways. First, as mentioned above, merchandising is a marketing tool. It generates recognition for recently launched television programs (although merchandise on retail shelves *too* early, before enough consumer awareness exists, will usually fail); it maintains ongoing awareness for long-term, classic series; and it can reinforce a network's brand image. Licensing allows the property owner to amplify and support other marketing efforts surrounding the show, such as trade and consumer advertising, on-air promotions, and retail tie-ins. It brings the brand and its message into retail environments, which are nontraditional venues for publicizing television shows. At the same time, licensed merchandise expands the total number of people who hear about or are reminded of the series through various advertising and promotional vehicles. In marketing parlance, this is known as multiplying the number of consumer/viewer impressions, and is an important goal.

Let's look at the example of *Tiny Toon Adventures,* a Steven Spielberg-produced animated series airing on the Fox Children's Network and licensed by Warner Bros. Consumer Products. Any on-air advertising messages directed at potential viewers of *Tiny Toons* are reinforced during shopping outings: at Toys R Us by plush toys; at the grocery store by fruit snacks; at Kmart by footwear, bedding, and apparel; just to name a few. Even if the child or his or her parent does not purchase any of these products, he or she is still being reminded of the show's existence repeatedly and in several different environments. And, if he or she does buy, say, a *Tiny Toons* backpack, the marketing message is continually reinforced to the child in his or her home, and to other kids that the child encounters while wearing or carrying the backpack.

The marketing muscle that merchandising can lend to a coordinated marketing plan becomes crucial as competition among different programs increases. The proliferation of new broadcast and cable networks—not to mention other entertainment vehicles such as video games, films, books, home videos, and the like—means that television executives need to take advantage of every opportunity to reinforce their brands and to create and maintain awareness for individual television programs.

The second benefit that merchandise licensing offers to property owners is a financial one. The economic aspect of licensing, like its potential marketing clout, is gaining significance in the eyes of the television community. As the cost of producing a television series rises, the money flowing from manufacturers to licensors in the form of royalty payments is an effective way to help offset these costs. In addition, a percentage of what is known as the "minimum guarantee"—payment due to the licensor regardless of sales levels—is normally paid up front as an advance, meaning that it can be put to use in financing the series well before merchandise hits store shelves.

To illustrate this concept with a hypothetical example, suppose a children's animated program based on a hit film is expected to generate licensed merchandise sales of about $200 million (at the retail level) over two years. This licensing program would be considered successful, but is certainly not out of the realm of possibility—*Barney & Friends*, for example, is estimated by various trade publications and industry observers to have driven retail sales of more than $500 million in products featuring Barney and his pal Baby Bop in just one year. The Teenage Mutant Ninja Turtles, meanwhile, have been responsible for more than $4 billion in retail sales worldwide since their birth as a licensed property in 1987, according to licensor Surge.

At the above-mentioned $200 million expected retail level, our hypothetical children's series could reasonably expect a guaranteed minimum royalty payment of approximately $7 million, with the potential for additional royalties at a rate of 7% of wholesale sales (with wholesale equaling about half of retail). About $880,000 of this could be payable as advances from all initial licensees together, assuming a rate of 25% of the first year's guarantees. (Royalty calculations are described in more detail in Chapter 4.)

If the series requires a production cost of $300,000 per episode, which is about average for children's animation in 1994, these figures mean that two full episodes could conceivably be financed by upfront money alone. Of course, royalty revenues—and guarantees and advances—vary widely. A brand-new property might not command the 7% royalty assumed in the hit-film-based example above, and in many cases guarantees and advances would be lower than they would be for this series, since demand for the property from manufacturers is a key consideration. This hypothetical situation does, however, demonstrate the financial assistance that a merchandising program could contribute to a series production effort. And, with costs escalating—*ReBoot*, a computer-animated series on ABC starting in the autumn of 1994, costs an estimated $500,000 an episode to make, according to reports in *Broadcasting & Cable* magazine—the potential economic contribution of a licensing effort must be taken seriously.

Another benefit of licensing from the point of view of the licensor—particularly owners of brands or classic characters—is trademark protection. In order to protect the value of a trademark, thereby preventing infringement, the property must be exploited in commerce. In other words, products incorporating the logo or character must be available for sale. Licensing is an effective method for television licensors (who are not, after all, manufacturers) to offer products to consumers.

So far we've examined the benefits of merchandising from the licensor's point of view. Why would a manufacturer, on the other hand, want to obtain the license for a television property, especially when required to pay advances and guarantees potentially in the tens of thousands of dollars (and occasionally even in the millions)? For one thing, associating a product line with a television show can be an effective marketing tool for licensees, just as it can be for companies in the television industry. A classic, long-airing television show—whether in reruns or well into a long first run—brings with it a brand identity and awareness that has been built up over the years. The licensee's products instantly gain the benefits of the brand association (in this case, the brand is a classic television show that consumers know and like). This immediate awareness comes without the huge investment by the manufacturer that would be required to launch its own brand from scratch.

For example, the products of an apparel maker who obtains the license to *Sesame Street* from the Children's Television Workshop are, in the eyes of consumers, part of the *Sesame Street* brand, a name that they value and associate with quality. The advances and royalties paid by the licensee are relatively insignificant when compared with the long-term investment that would be required for that company to launch its own brand. Furthermore, the brand benefits are realized instantly. A new brand would take years to nurture until it developed brand benefits similar to those that consumers already associate with Big Bird, Elmo, the Cookie Monster, and the rest of the *Sesame Street* neighborhood. In fact, there is no guarantee that customers would ever develop the same warm feeling—and perception of quality and value—for the apparel maker's own brand that they associate with CTW's trademarks. The same situation holds true for other established properties such as Nickelodeon, Disney, Looney Tunes, and so on.

Becoming linked with established television shows can also bring a built-in consumer base to a manufacturer's product. *Star Trek* is a good example of this; when a manufacturer takes the license for *Star Trek* on ties or dinnerware or apparel, that licensee knows that a certain core group of so-called "Trekkies" are likely to purchase that product. These consumers may, in fact, be unlikely to buy the same item without its *Star Trek* association. For instance, a certain *Star Trek* fan may not be a core consumer of water globes (remember those little glass-enclosed environments that you shake upside down to make it snow inside?). But when our Trekkie walks past a gift shop and sees a water globe manufactured by collectibles licensee Willitts Designs containing the *U.S.S. Enterprise*, the *Star Trek* spaceship, he or she may well make an impulse purchase.

The same situation holds true for other classic shows such as *M*A*S*H* or *I Love Lucy*, which have loyal core audiences. These shows do not generate billions of dollars in sales of licensed merchandise, but they could easily drive a nice business for a few manufacturers. *M*A*S*H* caps and limited-edition watches are available as of this writing, for example, and *I Love Lucy* has generated products ranging from trading cards to board games to collectible dolls.

Even brand-new shows without established awareness or a built-in consumer base can bring value to licensees. Associating with a new television show—as long as it is established enough to have garnered fans and consumer awareness—adds an element of fun and excitement to a product line. The graphics that are created in conjunction with these new series often lend themselves to fashion-forward, design-conscious products that can sell (sometimes even if the show is not top-rated). And, of course, there is always the potential with a new show that the licensee could be part of an unexpected home run, along the lines of *Teenage Mutant Ninja Turtles, Barney & Friends,* or *Mighty Morphin Power Rangers,* to name just a few recent merchandising hits. New properties are certainly riskier than the established shows (or brands) discussed above. Yet, for the licensee, they can be attractive because they are usually less costly than classic properties and they can still set the manufacturer's products apart from those of its competitors.

Finally, when a manufacturer obtains permission to utilize a television property—whether new or old—in conjunction with its products, it gains an additional marketing benefit. Not only does the television program itself act as an advertisement for the licensee's products, but the licensed merchandise from all the manufacturers tied in to the program promote each other. All the products contribute not just to potential viewers' awareness of the show, but to consumer recognition of the property and all the other merchandise associated with it. *Gargoyles* videocassettes promote *Gargoyles* party goods, which advertise *Gargoyles* action figures, which in turn support other products (Figure 1.1).

Risks of licensing

Despite all of these positive attributes for both licensing partners, entertainment merchandising programs are not without potential drawbacks. For licensees, the major risk, of course, is that the money that they owe to licensors in the form of guaranteed royalties may not be justified by increased sales levels. In other words, they might not recoup their investment.

In addition, if a licensee becomes associated with a property that somehow acquires a bad image, it may receive negative publicity, which could ultimately hurt its reputation. This situation would probably not occur because a television series is critically panned or low-rated, but rather because of a harder-to-fix image problem. A star who goes to prison or says something very controversial could indirectly hurt licensees of that star's television program (and its licensor, too). Licensees of live-action shows are more vulnerable than those of animation, since it is impossible to predict an actor's or actress's behavior in his or her personal life.

For licensors, the risk is not primarily a financial one, since they will receive, at the least, their minimum guarantees from all licensees. Their income from a merchandising effort can be significant, especially for properties that can command high guarantees or a large number of licensees. This incoming cash is safe, regardless of how the show performs or how many sales the licensing program generates. The risks for the licensor, rather, are image related and

FIGURE 1.1 The Buena Vista Television show *Gargoyles,* licensed by Disney Consumer Products. Each *Gargoyles* product helps promote other merchandise based on the property.

are often caused, at least partly, by mismanagement of the licensing program.

For example, overproliferation of products in the initial stages of the licensing program can stem any chance for long-term growth of merchandise sales and could, potentially, stunt the longevity of the show itself. The property becomes a fad, and when people become sick of it, it fades away, sometimes irretrievably. Of course, the television program itself does not *necessarily* end when sales of merchandise do, just as merchandise sales do not necessarily end when the show does. *The Simpsons* television show remained popular with viewers, despite the fact that the fad for Simpsons-related merchandise waned in the early '90s. As a matter of fact, after a hiatus, retail sales of Simpsons merchandise have picked up significantly to about $250 million annually, although they are unlikely to approach their $1 billion-plus peak annual level of 1991 (Figure 1.2). Still, as a rule, a faddish licensing program could be risky for the image of the series and ultimately its ratings.

Another, much bigger risk for the licensor is the possibility that inappropriate licensed products could harm the consumer's, and therefore the audience's, perception of the television show. A series that utilizes environmental themes within the program as a major marketing point (such as Turner's *Captain Planet* and others) may be hurt if environmentally harmful products—toys that are wrapped in a great deal of excess plastic packaging, as one possible example—are authorized and come to the attention of consumers. Such bad publicity could not only adversely affect sales of the merchandise, but could also undermine the credibility of the content and themes of the show itself.

Similarly, a children's educational show could be harmed if the licensing program becomes too large and consumers start to perceive that products based on it are purely commercial, without any educational value. Series airing on the PBS network or on local public television stations are especially susceptible to this charge, given the nonprofit, noncommercial nature of public television. Despite the fact that a portion of the revenues generated from a licensing effort usually goes back into the production of more quality programming, the potential for a consumer backlash due to the show's perceived overcommercialization still exists. People often seem to be adversely affected by what they consider to be too much commercialism more than they are swayed by the fact that merchandise sales are partially responsible for enabling more quality programming to be created.

MATT GROENING

FIGURE 1.2 *The Simpsons* merchandise peaked in the early '90s with total worldwide sales surpassing $2 billion. The show's continuing popularity enabled Twentieth Century Fox Licensing & Merchandising to relaunch the brand after a hiatus, and the property currently demonstrates strong annual sales levels.

Any children's licensing effort, whether the show is educational in nature or purely for entertainment, can be hurt if faulty products reach the marketplace. A plate containing toxic lead, a toy that has swallowable parts, a food product that makes kids sick—all of these hurt the licensing program and possibly the series itself. Obviously, such products should never be authorized, and vigilance and common sense on the part of the licensor go a long way toward preventing this harmful situation.

The possibility of hurting a property's image is an important concern for character-driven licensing programs, but it is truly a crucial one for branded licensing strategies. For owners of properties such as Nickelodeon, ABC Sports, The Cartoon Network, and others, the main reasons behind the merchandising effort are to help create and maintain awareness of the brand, and to enhance the brand's image to its current and potential viewers; these two goals override any potential financial gain. Avoiding any damage to the brand image due to inappropriate or faulty licensed merchandise is obviously of the utmost importance. These networks have invested millions of dollars to create and maintain their long-term brands, and licensing programs should support—and should absolutely never hurt—these trademarks.

An Overview of Television Licensing

Total retail sales of licensed entertainment and character merchandise reached $15.8 billion in the United States and Canada in 1993, according to *The Licensing Letter*, a trade publication that has tracked sales of licensed merchandise for more than fifteen years. Entertainment and character licensing includes television-related properties, in addition to merchandising programs based on films, classic characters (Mickey Mouse, Looney Tunes, Peanuts, etc.), and comic book characters.

It is difficult to assess the relative weight of television licensing as a subset of the broader entertainment segment, for two primary reasons. First, many licensable shows are based on properties that originally sprang from other media. The animated *X-Men* series currently airing on Fox is based on a Marvel comic; *The Busy World of Richard Scarry*—currently airing on Showtime and set for a concurrent run on Nickelodeon in 1995—is based on a book series; *Sonic the Hedgehog*, distributed in syndication, was engendered in a Sega video game, and so forth.

Secondly, a growing number of television series make up a single element of a larger overall entertainment franchise. It is thus difficult to directly trace sales of licensed merchandise back to the television vehicle, even if that is where the franchise started. To illustrate, of the more than $1.5 billion worth of Batman merchandise sold at retail worldwide since 1989, it is tough to determine how much is due to the current animated series airing on Fox—as opposed to the animated film, the three live-action films, the original comic books, possibly even the 1960s series, and so on. The same situation exists for other television-related franchises, including *Star Trek*, the Ninja Turtles, *The Little Mermaid*, and others. So, instead of examining television licensing as a distinct segment, it is worthwhile to look at it as one integral component of the larger entertainment and character merchandising field.

To put the entertainment and character licensing segment in a larger context, more merchandise sales are attributable to this type of property than to any other single area of licensing, according to *The Licensing Letter*. In 1993, within the total $66.6 billion North American market for licensed merchandise, *TLL* estimates that entertainment and character properties accounted for 23.7% of total retail sales of licensed products, followed by sports with 19.7%, corporate trademarks and brands with 19%, and fashion labels with 17.7%. Other types of licensable properties with smaller shares of the total include art, celebrities and estates, music, non-profit groups, publishing, and toys and games.

A brief history of television licensing

Merchandise licensing is not a new phenomenon in the television industry. *Howdy Doody* in the 1950s, *Star Trek* in the 1960s, and *The Six-Million Dollar Man* in the 1970s are just a few of the television-based properties responsible for the creation of toys, banks, lunch boxes, T-shirts, and many other consumer products. Many of these licensed items from the '50s through the '70s are sought-after and pricey collectibles today.

In the late '70s, an event occurred that—while not directly related to television—greatly affected entertainment licensing as a whole, including efforts based on television shows. The release of the first *Star Wars* feature film spawned a significant licensing program, led by toy licensee Kenner. In fact, the *Star Wars* trilogy was responsible for more than $2.5 billion worth of retail sales of licensed products over a six-year period in the late '70s and early '80s, according to its licensor, Lucasfilm. Lucasfilm still oversees an active licensing program, in fact, with successful products on the market, including trading cards, electronics, a best-selling book series, and many others.

Retail sales of licensed merchandise in 1977 were a fraction of what they are today, according to *The Licensing Letter*, accounting for just $4.9 billion in retail sales across all property types. The *Star Wars* phenomenon is widely considered the point at which entertainment licensing began to grow exponentially; it indicated to marketers that licensed properties, particularly of the toy-driven children's entertainment variety, were potentially big business.

The 1980s marked an explosion of television-related licensed properties. Some, such as *ALF*, *Dynasty*, and *The Smurfs* (ubiquitous on children's products in 1983, generating an estimated half billion dollars at retail), all originated as television series and spawned a wide variety of merchandise. Other properties in that decade drove major licensing efforts once they were developed into television series. *He-Man and Masters of the Universe* was originally based on a toy line from Mattel. *Care Bears*, which generated more than $1 billion in retail sales of licensed merchandise, was created by a licensing company called Those Characters From Cleveland, a subsidiary of American Greetings. And the *Ghostbusters* television show in the late 1980s was based on a series of live-action films that were released earlier that decade. Television-driven properties were responsible for a significant portion of the entertainment licensing business in the '80s; these examples are just a few of the myriad properties of note.

In the 1990s, licensing is a maturing business. That is, its growth curve is starting to level off from the double-digit increases seen throughout the 1980s. This is not to say that the size of the market is declining; on the contrary. And, while the nature of licensing is changing (as we'll see in Chapter 2), blockbuster merchandising programs are certainly still possible.

The year 1990, for example, was notable for home-run television-related properties. *The Simpsons* generated over $1 billion in worldwide retail sales in a single fiscal year, according to licensor Twentieth Century Fox. The same year also marked the peak of popularity for the *Teenage Mutant Ninja Turtles*, a multi-billion-dollar property that continues to generate sales of toys and other products as of this writing.

Beverly Hills 90210 and *Thomas the Tank Engine* in 1992, *Barney & Friends* in 1993, and the *Mighty Morphin Power Rangers* in 1994 are all into the hundreds of millions of dollars in total retail sales of licensed products, and continue to drive merchandise purchases. The 1990s are also notable, however, not just for blockbusters but for the number of different types of licensed properties available. Niche opportunities such as *Northern Exposure* may not be home runs, but can be beneficial for small groups of licensees. Long-term branded opportunities such as MTV offer licensees the opportunity to be associated with a property that is recognized by their target customers (in this case teens). Even Saturday morning interstitials, the 30- or 60-second bumpers that run between weekend kids' shows (*Stickin' Around* is an example) are sometimes available for licensing. Television programs targeted to all age groups are increasingly viewed as having licensing potential. We'll discuss this further in Chapter 2.

It should also be noted that while the overall trend in entertainment licensing is steady but not exponential growth, the business is by nature cyclical. Total sales of licensed merchandise rise and fall depending on the number of strong properties available and whether or not they strike a chord with consumers. For example, a peak in total sales of licensed merchandise occurred in the late '70s with *Star Wars*. The mid-'80s marked another high point, with *The Smurfs*, Cabbage Patch Kids dolls, *Masters of the Universe*, *Strawberry Shortcake*, and others. The most recent turn of the decade, with *The Simpsons*, the Ninja Turtles, and the singing group New Kids On The Block, was also a peak. Between each of these big years, however, were valleys, during which lower sales levels occurred. This is the nature of entertainment licensing.

An Overview of Television Licensing Possibilities

Most of the top-selling examples noted above are character-driven licensing programs targeted at children, many based on animation. This type of licensing will continue to make up a large portion of the business—most of the programs approaching or even surpassing $1 billion in retail sales will be from this category, certainly. Kids' animation properties will continue to garner much of the publicity, as well.

Why will these properties continue to dominate television-related licensing? First of all, children are a large portion of the entertainment merchandise-buying public, or at least exert a lot of influence over the actual purchasers. In fact, Dr. James McNeal of Texas A&M University, as reported in *Youth Markets Alert*, estimates that children ages four to twelve spend $11 billion annually, and influence more than $160 billion more in family purchases.

Much of their influence is directed at licensed products—*The Licensing Letter* estimates that 65% to 70% of all entertainment and character-licensed merchandise is purchased for or by children. Adults, on the other hand, may be loyal fans of a particular show but they are often less inclined to translate their feelings for the television series into a merchandise purchase. For this reason, a licensing program usually must appeal to children to achieve blockbuster status.

In addition, kids' programs with readily identifiable characters, particularly animated or costumed ones, lend themselves well to merchandise applications. The Walt Disney animated film and television character Aladdin, for example, can be applied to all sorts of merchandise in graphically interesting and colorfully appealing ways—and new art incorporating the blue genie can be created by Disney for such purposes. On the other hand, it is more difficult to take archival stills of the cast of *Green Acres* and create the same range of different styles of merchandise (not to mention the difficulty that can occur in negotiating rights with the talent or their estates). The flexibility to apply unique graphic representations to a wide variety of merchandise is virtually always required for a billion-dollar property. Licensees across product categories need to attract repeat sales of merchandise in order to accumulate huge numbers; the creation of fresh products is one major way to do this. Customers are not likely to buy graphically similar merchandise over and over.

While animation will continue to drive the majority of the largest and most visible licensing programs, there is certainly also potential for some live-action shows to achieve comparable sales. *Star Trek* and *Mighty Morphin Power Rangers* are examples of home-run licensing programs based on live-action shows. In addition, there are niche opportunities for a number of live-action series. These properties fall into two major categories—some are nostalgic, while others are currently on the air.

Nostalgic licensing efforts tend to appeal to core fans of a series, either in its original version or via reruns in syndication or on cable. The series that are currently airing in reruns attract new, younger fans in addition to older viewers who continue to watch the series primarily for its nostalgic value. Nostalgic licensing programs usually focus for the most part on collectibles (trading cards, mugs, figurines, and so forth) and some apparel and accessory items, such as T-shirts and caps. In addition to these core categories, products with a close association to the show's themes are sometimes created. Viacom, for example, the licensor of *The Andy Griffith Show*, has licensed a cookbook based on recipes that the character Aunt Bee might have used to make meals in the fictional town of Mayberry, in addition to more traditional categories.

While not every nostalgic licensing program is a coordinated effort like the one centering on *Andy Griffith*, several licensors have authorized a few individual product lines for nostalgic television shows. *The Twilight Zone*, *The Brady Bunch*, *Gilligan's Island*, *The Honeymooners*, and many others are all available for licensing and have been responsible for at least one or two product lines.

Niche licensing programs based on current shows usually focus on products that emulate the lifestyle portrayed on the television program, although some collectibles are often authorized as well. For example, *thirtysomething* engendered a line of apparel that the characters in the program might wear, targeted at the baby boomers who enjoyed the show, while *Blossom* sprouted apparel, accessories, and other products for pre-teen and teen girls.

Another illustration of a lifestyle-related niche program is *Beverly Hills 90210*, targeted at teens and pre-teens and featuring apparel incorporating the show's logo, as well as other products (including a line of fashion dolls from Mattel bearing the likenesses of the show's characters). As mentioned earlier, this effort ended up exceeding expectations for a niche program, with retail sales topping $250 million in the United States, according to its licensing agent, Hamilton Projects. The property's international program has approached a similar sales level.

Several popular comedies also have engendered product lines made up of what are known as "social expressions"—that is, merchandise that incorporates catch phrases or jokes from the show, such as greeting cards, posters, mugs, and T-shirts. *Home Improvement*, *Coach*, and *Seinfeld* are three examples. Daytime soap operas such as *All My Children* and several others are also active in the social expressions area.

All of the licensing activities cited so far are show-specific, centering on one television series and its logos, characters, graphics, or the lifestyle portrayed on it. Another significant—and growing—area of television-related licensing, however, includes those efforts focusing on network brands. These merchandising programs are, in general, very conservative, targeted closely toward the broadcast or cable network's core audience. In fact, it is licensors of exactly these brands and sub-brands—those that do have a core audience with identifiable characteristics—who are able to successfully launch this type of licensing effort. Some of the many examples that currently exist of branded merchandising programs include those launched by HBO, CNN, and Nickelodeon. Merchandise licensing efforts focusing on network sub-brands—that is, not the network name itself, but programming blocks identified by a separate umbrella logo—include Nick at Nite, ABC Sports, and the *NBA on NBC*. All of these branded programs are characterized by a narrow range of product categories, very careful selection of licensees, and slow expansion. As mentioned earlier, the overriding objective of branded licensing efforts is to support the brand image in the minds of the viewers and consumers—and, even more importantly, to not *harm* the brand in any way. Thus, these licensors necessarily tend to develop extremely conservative licensing strategies.

Merchandising programs of all these types—niche and branded licensing efforts, as well as the more traditional animated kids' series with blockbuster potential—will continue to proliferate throughout the 1990s and beyond. Chapter 2 will examine several of the larger trends that are responsible for this diversification in television licensing.

Chapter 2

Current Trends in Broadcast and Cable Licensing

The Maturation of the U.S. Licensing Business

The licensing business in the United States and Canada—that is, the business conducted by licensees and licensors across a wide variety of industries (entertainment, sports, apparel, toys, and dozens of others)—is maturing. Over the past ten years, licensing has become recognized by marketers on both sides of the merchandising equation for its ability to generate revenues and to build and maintain awareness of a television show or brand. In the 1990s, however, after nearly fifteen years of exponential growth, licensed merchandise sales overall are increasing more slowly than they did in the late 1970s and the 1980s. The size of the licensing business should continue to rise, as more participants in many industries realize the potential of merchandising as a marketing tool. Double-digit growth, however, is most likely a thing of the past.

With this maturation comes an increasing level of sophistication throughout the business, on the part of both licensees and licensors. Licensing is no longer viewed as simply a way to make lots of money in a short time, but rather as a potentially effective tool for both licensor and licensee within the context of their respective marketing plans.

This realization affects those within the licensing community—who have been associated with merchandising for many years—

and those throughout the larger business community—some of whom may be looking at licensing for the first time. Increasing sophistication means that publicity-generating blockbusters in the vein of *Jurassic Park* are not the only option. The potential home runs will still exist, of course, and many marketers will probably continue to pin their hopes on such programs. Some of those hopes will be realized.

At the same time, however, smaller niche and branded merchandising efforts are proliferating. Licensors are increasingly examining the merchandising potential of *all* of their properties, and licensees are more often viewing smaller, non-blockbuster licenses as effective for them. While these smaller properties will not drive billions of dollars worth of licensed merchandise sales, they can provide a good fit with individual product lines. Thus, they have the potential to become a strong marketing tool for their respective licensors' and licensees' specific needs.

In terms of television licensing specifically, this trend is causing an increasing number of licensors with television properties to look at merchandising as a viable alternative for creating awareness and recouping investments. Many of those who never thought of their properties as being merchandisable in the past are now analyzing each television program to see if any licensing relationships—even just one or two per show—make sense. Cable networks, syndicators, independent producers, and the major broadcast networks are all increasing their participation.

Increased Competition within the Television Industry

Changes in the television industry are also spurring the active participation of more television property owners in licensing. Increased competition within the television industry is a primary influence, of course. New broadcast networks launched by Viacom (which recently purchased Paramount) and Warner Bros. in 1995 add to the already competitive arena of broadcast television. The relatively recent addition of the Fox network to the fray was a significant development in terms of licensing; Fox has developed into a major player within the last few years, becoming a dominant distribution channel for not only children's animation, but licensable adult properties, including *The Simpsons*, *Married . . . With Chil-*

dren, Melrose Place, and many others. It is too soon to say, at this writing, exactly what effect the entry of Paramount and Warner will have on the television industry or the licensing business, but increased competition for viewers and dollars is certainly a likely outcome. This competition will occur not only among the six broadcast networks—ABC, CBS, NBC, Fox, United/Paramount, and Warner—but also among the ever-increasing number of individual shows aired on these networks.

A parallel trend toward more competition is occurring within the syndication market. The development of programming blocks such as the Disney Afternoon or Bohbot's Amazing Adventures blocks for boys' and girls' programming makes it more difficult for smaller, independent companies to get their shows on the air in syndication. The partnership between Fox and Warner—which continues through 1997—for blocks of animation on the Fox Children's Network also adds to this difficulty. Competition among independent programmers and their syndicators to get their shows on the air has heated up, and will in all likelihood continue to do so, despite the fact that more channels of distribution are being created.

In the cable business (both basic and pay channels), meanwhile, more networks are being launched each year. This increased competition from new additions such as the Sci-Fi Channel and the Cartoon Network drives cable marketers to search for additional ways to differentiate their brands. They want to stop channel surfing by viewers, and thus increase their ratings. As networks proliferate, it is ever more important to avoid getting lost in the clutter. And, as we enter the much-talked-about 500-channel world of the future, the issue of brand differentiation will continue to grow in importance.

A final addition to the litany of competitive pressures comes from outside traditional television providers. It should be remembered that other types of video entertainment are increasingly vying with television for viewers' time, most notably home video and video games. The latter is currently a $3.97 billion market at the wholesale level, according to the Toy Manufacturers of America, including hardware and software purchases. Similarly, the home video market has burgeoned. According to Veronis, Suhler & Associates' *Communications Industry Forecast* (seventh edition), spending on video rentals surpassed $8 billion in 1992, and purchases of videocassettes reached $3.7 billion. Time spent with either of these video entertainment vehicles cuts into the time spent watching traditional television programming. Television viewing still dominates these other video-related activities, at least for younger children—the average child aged two to eleven watches about twenty-one hours of television per week versus 2.5 hours of videos and .7 hours on video games, according to the report. Still, as more players are competing for a share of this television-viewing time, not only is the pie being divided into more and smaller pieces, but its size could shrink.

What does this increased competition in the broadcast, syndication, and cable markets mean for television-based merchandise licensing? First, more competition means an increasingly fragmented viewership and fan base. As a result, the likelihood of blockbuster licensing programs may decrease as the number of fans for any individual show—and thus the number of potential consumers of licensed merchandise—declines. This is not to say that blockbusters won't occur, however. Licensing is unpredictable, and a blockbuster may still create its own momentum, regardless of its small-segment origin.

Secondly, a rise in competition means that the number of potentially licensable properties will multiply. More programs will become available as potential distribution channels proliferate; meanwhile, television property owners will more often merchandise their shows and brands as a means of generating awareness.

Brands and Sub-Brands Increasingly Licensed

One trend that has strengthened as a result of these changes in the licensing and television businesses is the growth of merchandising efforts centering on network brands, as opposed to individual programs or characters. As mentioned in Chapter 1, licensing can be an effective way to support a brand-differentiation strategy, if the merchandising program is well managed and selective. The brands that are particularly apt for licensing efforts are those whose target audience is well defined.

In the network area, ABC has overseen several such branded programs. Examples include ABC Sports' licensing program, which incorporates *Wide World of Sports* and *Monday Night Football* merchandise appealing primarily to men, and the ABC Daytime brand, which includes the daytime soap opera *All My Children* and others. This program is targeted primarily toward women and college students, and while much of the merchandise is show-specific, it is all identified under the ABC Daytime brand umbrella. NBC has also experimented with brand licensing, launching a program for NBC Sports, the *NBA on NBC*, and the NBC Peacock logo.

Several cable networks have implemented branded licensing programs, as well. Nickelodeon, in fact, was a pioneer in this area, and oversees programs for the Nickelodeon brand, targeted toward ages six to eleven, as well as sub-brands Nick at Nite for adults, Nick Jr. for ages two to five, and others. Similarly, MTV hopes its merchandising program will support the network's image by incorporating the on-air logos and graphics for which it is famous into apparel and gifts. Turner's Cartoon Network has also launched a branded program, as have ESPN, HBO, CNN, and others.

It should be noted that some difficulties associated with this type of licensing program do exist, in spite of the potential for building awareness, supporting brand image, generating ancillary revenues, and differentiating a network from its competitors. No matter how much identification viewers feel with a certain network, for instance, there is no guarantee that they will demonstrate that loyalty by purchasing products. Furthermore, it can be difficult to translate a brand image into merchandise, and to keep the product lines fresh enough to generate continued purchases over a long time period. At this writing, both CNN and MTV are currently in the process of reassessing and relaunching their licensing programs after first announcing them two to three years ago. They still acknowledge the potential of licensing as a way to support their brand images; the best strategy to achieve this, however, can require fine-tuning.

Increased Cable Participation in Licensing

As noted, many cable networks are examining branded licensing programs as viable marketing and revenue-generating opportunities. Another development, however, is the fact that these networks are also more often looking at their own original programming for merchandising potential. The amount of original programming on cable networks is growing. In its early days, cable used to be primarily an outlet for reruns, classic films, and other acquired program-ming. Lately, however, these networks are commissioning or co-producing original programming for first-run distribution. And, since the networks often participate in the financing of these shows, they look to recoup some of their investment through merchandis-ing revenues.

Nickelodeon has licensed several of its original programs, in-cluding *Eureeka's Castle*, *Ren & Stimpy*, *Doug*, *Rugrats*, and others, and is planning merchandising programs for several upcoming series as well. MTV, of course, had a much-noted success with *Beavis & Butt-head* starting in 1993, and is planning to merchandise other series, such as *The Brothers Grunt*. USA Network (with its sister company Viacom Consumer Products) is, as of this writing, experimenting on a limited scale with *Duckman* (Figure 2.1) and *Itsy-Bitsy Spider*; Turner's TBS (with its sister company Turner Home Entertainment) licenses its series *2 Stupid Dogs* and *S.W.A.T. Kats*; the Discovery Channel has licensed its aviation series *Wings* for a line of replica planes based on footage from the series.

In addition to original programming and network-owned trademarks, several shows acquired by cable networks are also licensed, of course. These include nostalgic programming such as *The Dick Van Dyke Show* or *The Honeymooners*, as well as acquired first-run shows such as *The Mighty Jungle* on The Family Channel and *The Busy World of Richard Scarry* on Showtime and Nickel-odeon. The motivating force behind these licensing efforts is usu-ally the property owner or its licensing agent, rather than the cable network. Acquired cable programs are significant to this discus-sion, however, in that they demonstrate that cable-aired shows are increasingly considered to have licensing potential. Five to ten years ago, and still today to some extent, the broadcast networks were thought to be the best outlet for a licensed property. This is beginning to change, however; broadcast is still an important dis-tribution channel, but it is no longer considered crucial to a success-ful licensing program, thanks to cable's growing viability.

Another related development is the fact that several cable-aired shows, particularly those in first-run, are the focus of dual distribu-tion. That is, they are aired on two cable networks—or sometimes broadcast or syndication and cable—at once, either simultaneously or with a season or two lag time. The Richard Scarry program, mentioned above, is one example, as is *The Adventures of Tintin*, on HBO and Nickelodeon. This trend makes cable shows even more

FIGURE 2.1   *Duckman*, an animated series airing on the USA Network, is an example of original cable programming available for licensing. Viacom Consumer Products represents the property.

attractive from a licensing perspective, because they attract a larger and more diverse audience.

There are several reasons for the increased participation of cable networks in merchandising. First, licensing programs for defined audiences are becoming more attractive to marketers of all types as they try to segment their consumers more narrowly, in the hopes of targeting them more accurately. Second, increased competition for slots on broadcast, combined with more airtime available on cable outlets, means that more licensable properties find their way to cable. Third, fragmentation in both the broadcast and cable marketplace allows cable audiences, while still often smaller than network viewerships, to be considered viable. Fourth, cable's total viewing audience is growing—cable currently has a 25.8% viewing share, according to a Paul Kagan Associates/Advanstar report, and

Nickelodeon says it reaches 34% of all kids' viewership each week, more than the networks and syndication combined. This increasing audience makes cable shows more attractive for licensing. And finally, cable merchandising efforts have proven to be commercially profitable—MTV's *Beavis & Butt-head* and Nickelodeon's *Ren & Stimpy* are two recent examples.

Niche Licensing Programs on the Rise

The increasing appeal of cable programming and brands reflects a larger trend in television licensing, as well: namely, that niche licensing programs are proliferating, as mentioned earlier. Niche licensing is defined as the act of targeting a merchandising program toward a narrowly defined core audience, not expecting a blockbuster but rather a relatively small number of lines that meet the goals of both licensee and licensor. The television programs that work best are those that have a loyal viewership and that have thematic or graphical elements that lend themselves well to merchandise. Both nostalgic and current programming can be developed into niche licensing efforts. *Home Improvement* (Figure 2.2), *I Love Lucy*, *The X-Files*, *Trailside: Make Your Own Adventure*, *The Road*, *M*A*S*H*, *L.A. Law*, *NYPD Blue*, *Wheel of Fortune*, and *Rescue 911* are just some of the many examples of television programs that have spawned merchandise lines.

While many people evaluate children's programs solely as possible blockbusters—thinking that a show either has blockbuster potential or no potential at all—niche efforts are also possible here. The science themes of *Beakman's World*, for instance, translate to products such as games and activity toys, extending the show's educational mission off-air.

Similarly, *Bill Nye the Science Guy* has been featured on T-shirts and other products taking advantage of both the wacky humor of the show and its science education themes. Children's Television Workshop's *Ghostwriter* is licensed for a series of books, computer software, and other products that support the show's reading and writing themes. *Mr. Rogers' Neighborhood* has a small ongoing licensing effort as well; products include a replica of the wooden trolley car featured in the series and plush puppets based on the series' characters.

These shows all lend themselves to products that have a specific tie-in with the series, but are not perceived by their licensors as

FIGURE 2.2 *Home Improvement*, a Touchstone Television production that has generated licensed products including trading cards, greeting cards, and other merchandise. Disney Consumer Products handles licensing.
© Touchstone Pictures & Television. Photo Credit: Jonathan Exley.

being appropriate for every product category. They will most likely never achieve blockbuster status, but licensees who are able to logically associate with them can be successful.

A number of niche properties in recent years have focused on the pre-teen, or "tween," girls' market. A major impetus for this trend was the merchandising success of *Beverly Hills 90210*, as well as the prior success of the singing group New Kids On The Block, who racked up about $800 million in retail sales of merchandise in 1990. Both licensing programs were launched to target girls 8–12, focusing mainly on apparel and accessories. After they became successful within the pre-teen market, the licensing programs were expanded downward demographically and products for younger girls, such as fashion dolls, paper party goods, and so on, were added.

Both of these licensing programs transcended niche licensing and developed into home runs. Their success, however, led to a number of other television properties targeting the same market, girls aged 8–12, including *California Dreams, Saved By The Bell,* and many others. Some of these licensing programs were short-lived— as were the television shows—but are still notable in that they illustrate the growing viability of niche-oriented merchandising efforts in the minds of television and licensing executives.

Changes in Financial Interest and Syndication Rules

The major impetus behind all of the trends discussed thus far is increased competition within the licensing and television businesses. But regulatory issues also have an effect on television licensing. One of the most significant recently is the Federal Communications Commission's ending of its financial interest and syndication rules (fin-syn) in late 1993, and the almost-simultaneous striking down of the Justice Department's antitrust consent decrees, which had largely the same restrictions as fin-syn.

The fin-syn rules were adopted in the early 1970s. They restricted the major broadcast networks, ABC, NBC, and CBS (Fox and the other new networks are not affected), from producing in-house more than 40 percent of their prime-time schedules; prevented them from taking a financial stake in the shows on their schedules provided by outside producers; and disallowed them from syndicating any of their own programs, thus eliminating the possibility of back-end syndication revenues.

The relaxation of the rules immediately enabled the networks to own a portion of their acquired shows and to increase the amount of in-house programming that they produce. In addition, it will allow them to enter the syndication market in 1995, unless various challenges to the ruling are successful prior to then (which industry observers think is unlikely).

How does the end of fin-syn affect licensing? The first result is the increased participation of ABC, NBC, and CBS in the licensing field, which is already beginning to occur and is anticipated to increase. Some of the networks did dabble in licensing prior to the changes, as noted earlier, with their own brands. With the end of fin-syn, however, the networks can participate in the upfront financing of shows, so they naturally want to recoup their investment on the back end through syndication or, more to the point here, through merchandising.

Early signs of increased participation are already evident. CBS Enterprises recently hired its first VP of Licensing & Merchandising, for example, indicating its intention to exploit its owned shows—including *Dr. Quinn, Medicine Woman*; *Dave's World*; and *Walker, Texas Ranger*—through licensing where it makes financial or marketing sense. ABC, meanwhile, commissioned its first wholly owned children's program, premiering in the fall of 1994, the stop-action animated series *Bump In The Night*. The network, in association with DIC Merchandising, is aggressively pursuing licensing deals—this is the first Saturday morning series for which it has done so—and so far has signed licensees for books, bedding, Halloween costumes, and other products. ABC is also handling syndication, international distribution, home video, and musical recordings for *Bump*, in addition to licensing, all thanks in large part to the elimination of fin-syn.

Bump In The Night illustrates another probable effect on licensing that may well result from the relaxation of the FCC's fin-syn rules. ABC, because of its financial interest in the series, has given it a two-year commitment—far longer than the average commitment for a new series, although not entirely unknown. This support is important. It gives the show time to catch on with viewers even if it is not popular right out of the box. It also allows the licensing program to roll out slowly instead of saturating the market, giving it a greater chance for a long life. And, the increased commitment makes the show more attractive to potential licensees, since it eliminates the risk of early cancellation.

Some observers believe that the increased financial flexibility that the end of fin-syn allows means that some shows will now reach the airwaves that would not have had a chance prior to the end of the FCC rules. Some of these shows may have licensing potential.

A related development is the fact that—while broadcast networks are looking to increase their financial ownership of programming—producers are looking for partners to help share costs. As production costs rise—the Saban series *V.R. Troopers* reportedly costs about $750,000 per episode—independent producers and Hollywood studios are looking for partners, such as the networks, to help defray upfront costs. In return, they often give up some of the back-end financial gains from syndication and merchandising.

The networks' participation in licensing is limited at present in a couple of ways. First, they do not, at this point, have the same level of expertise in licensing as other long-time participants, such as some independent production companies, the major Hollywood studios, and others in the industry. Therefore, they will be likely to enter merchandising in conjunction with more experienced partners, at least in the short term (just as ABC is doing with DIC).

Secondly, and more importantly, the networks do not want to compete with the Hollywood community to the detriment of their existing relationships. By aggressively competing with independent producers to fill time slots—and for licensing revenues—they could jeopardize their relationships with the creative community on whom they continue to depend for programming. In fact, independent producers are largely viewed as the group most threatened by the end of fin-syn. Thus, the networks walk a fine line between taking full advantage of their assets and not offending those with whom they want to maintain continuing relationships.

The end of the financial interest and syndication rules is affecting television licensing in other related ways, in addition to providing the impetus for further network participation in licensing. One major effect is that, as the broadcast networks increase their involvement in licensing, syndication, and production as their financial ownership in programming grows, smaller independent companies already in these businesses are feeling the added competitive pressure, as noted earlier.

As a result, many independent producers and syndicators are looking to expand their businesses outside their traditional niches. One possibility under frequent consideration is to take a more active role in the licensing field. By representing properties with which they are associated as producers or syndicators (or both), as well as acting as licensing agents for third-party properties, these smaller companies can enhance their bottom lines. Several organizations have recently diversified by setting up dedicated licensing or consumer products divisions.

One example is Bohbot Entertainment, which describes itself as a "youth-oriented marketing services company specializing in media planning and buying, syndication, licensing and merchandising, promotions, public relations and special events." The "licensing and merchandising" aspect is relatively new; the company recently launched a consumer products division to handle licensing activities for the programming it syndicates, including *Double Dragon, Princess Gwenevere and the Jewel Riders, Highlander,* and others.

Similarly, ITC Entertainment, a producer and distributor of feature films, television movies, and television programming, recently consolidated its licensing activities, named a VP of Licensing, and hired additional licensing staff to coordinate worldwide merchandising efforts based on its 10,000-plus hours of television and film programming, including *Thunderbirds* (Figure 2.3), *Captain Scarlet*, and others. These series have been licensed in the past— *Thunderbirds* has surpassed $350 million in retail sales of licensed merchandise worldwide—but this consolidation and expansion demonstrates ITC's intention to become more active in the licensing business.

And Lancit Media, producers of *The Puzzle Place*, among other shows, also recently increased its participation in licensing by purchasing 85% of The Strategy Licensing Company, a licensing agency. Strategy represents some of Lancit's programs, including *Puzzle Place*, as well as third-party properties.

FIGURE 2.3 Virgil, Gordon, and Alan, three of the puppet stars of ITC's *Thunderbirds*, a nostalgic series being relaunched for broadcast and for licensing. Courtesy of ITC Entertainment Group Ltd. *Thunderbirds*™ and © 1995 ITC Entertainment Group Ltd. All rights reserved.

While several factors play a role in these companies' decision to expand into or become more active in merchandising—including several of the trends discussed earlier in the chapter—the FCC's elimination of financial-syndication rules is certainly one important impetus.

The FCC, Children's Programming, and the Influence of PBS

One of the most visible trends in television licensing in the early to mid-1990s has been the increasing influence of public television in driving licensed merchandise sales. Of course, the Children's Television Workshop's *Sesame Street*, which celebrated its 25th anniversary in 1994, is among the top-selling classic licenses year in and year out, generating $800 million per year on average in retail sales, according to industry experts cited in *Broadcasting*. *Sesame Street*, however, was previously considered something of an aberration in the licensing business. Despite its success, most manufacturers shied away from "educational" programming and PBS in particular. Programming of this nature was generally perceived as having too small an audience to drive lucrative licensed merchandise efforts.

That viewpoint changed in the early 1990s. First Thomas the Tank Engine, the star of PBS's *Shining Time Station* (produced by Britt Allcroft), was featured on much-in-demand merchandise for pre-schoolers. Then Barney the purple dinosaur, star of The Lyons Group's *Barney & Friends*, found himself in the same situation starting in the fourth quarter of 1992. These two properties, along with *Sesame Street* and other currently licensed PBS properties, are estimated by *The Licensing Letter* to have driven more than $1.5 billion in retail sales of merchandise in 1993.

Initially, licensors of both of these properties had a hard time convincing manufacturers of their sales potential. It was only after a grassroots surge of popularity from kids ages 2 to 4—and the fact that their parents began bombarding retailers with requests for merchandise—that these became sought-after properties in the eyes of retail buyers and potential licensees.

By 1994 Thomas and Barney, along with the gang from *Sesame Street*, had proven to the licensing and television communities that educational series—especially those distributed by PBS and aimed at pre-schoolers—do have commercial potential. A great number of current and upcoming PBS shows, for pre-schoolers and school-age children, are available for licensing and are, as of this writing, attracting a great deal of demand from manufacturers. A partial list includes *The Magic School Bus, Storytime, Puzzle Place, Lamb Chop's Play-Along,* and *Kratt's Creatures.* Other PBS shows with smaller licensing efforts include *Mr. Rogers' Neighborhood* and *Ghostwriter.*

PBS has received some flack in press reports and government hearings for the relatively low income it has received from the merchandising of PBS series, in spite of the seeming ubiquity of products based on some of them. In fact, according to a report in *Broadcasting,* the Corporation for Public Broadcasting received only $317,000 in merchandising revenues in 1991. This sum is in contrast to the fact that, on retail sales of $1.5 billion, royalties of approximately $52 million would accrue, at a 7% royalty rate. Using these hypothetical figures—the $1.5 billion sales figure is probably somewhat high for 1991, which was prior to the height of Thomas and Barney—less than 1% of total merchandising revenues went back to PBS. This situation is changing, however, as PBS renegotiates its arrangements with the series' producers to receive a more equitable portion of licensing royalties in return for its upfront financial assistance.

In addition to these PBS programs, a similar group of shows with licensing potential exists. These are series that air on PBS affiliate stations, who acquire them from distributors other than PBS, primarily the Boston-based American Program Service. These series, which include *Dudley the Dragon* (Figure 2.4), *Kidsongs,* and *Pappyland,* are also viewed as having licensing potential, as long as they reach adequate levels of household coverage across the country.

Meanwhile, so-called "edutainment" properties (those containing both educational elements and entertainment value) on commercial networks are also on the rise. Increasing interest on the part of the FCC in children's programming, including its investigation into how to best encourage compliance with 1990's Children's Television Act, are causing more producers to create shows with educational value, and causing more networks and stations to be interested in carrying them.

Whether the FCC enacts a rule requiring broadcasters to air a certain amount of educational programming or if, instead, the television community voluntarily self-regulates by upping the amount

FIGURE 2.4 Dudley the Dragon with his friends Sally and Matt. Dudley stars in a series distributed on public television stations. Licensed products include apparel, toys, and many others.

© 1994 Dragon Tales Productions, Inc. Under license by Meridian Direct, Inc.

of children's educational programming without any legislation being enacted, the result will be an increase in edutainment, whether delivered on PBS, on broadcast or cable networks, or in syndication.

As a greater number of educational shows are created, it follows that more will be available for licensing. This has already begun to occur. As of mid-1993, numerous "FCC-friendly" programs, in addition to the public television shows enumerated above, are being offered for licensing. Not only are they available, but their licensors are using their educational elements and FCC-friendliness as a marketing hook. Just a few of these properties at this writing include *Johnson & Friends*, an Australian pre-school series airing on Fox; *Dinobabies*, a Fred Wolf Films production; and *Old McDonald's Farm*, produced by DIC and airing on Lifetime.

The success of the *Mighty Morphin Power Rangers* is one indication that pure entertainment properties are not going to be wholly replaced in the marketplace by FCC-friendly ones. In addition, an overproliferation of FCC-friendliness will ultimately lead to a weeding out of weaker properties. Still, recent developments mean that educational television shows will continue to be assessed for their merchandising potential. Not every FCC-friendly series will be commercially successful—not all will be able to attract viewers (or advertisers, if on commercial networks) and not all will have merchandising success—but they will certainly not be dismissed out of hand as virtually doomed to fail economically.

It is interesting to note, by the way, that some local PBS affiliates are also increasing their participation in licensing. Both KCET in Los Angeles and WGBH in Boston have recently formed licensing divisions, for example. KCET is a partner in the production of the pre-school series *Puzzle Place*. Interestingly, WGBH is known for its non-children's programming and is beginning to tap into the trends discussed earlier in this chapter by licensing out such series as *NOVA*, *Victory Garden*, and *This Old House* for product lines closely related to the themes of the respective shows.

Blurring of the Lines between Television, Films, and Other Entertainment

Another trend greatly affecting television licensing is the blurring of the lines between various entertainment vehicles. Individual licensed properties are increasingly exploited across all media—television, film, video games, home video, books, magazines, comics, and so on—in order to lengthen their life spans and keep them fresh over time. Thus, the line between a television property versus a film property versus a video-game property, and so forth, is increasingly fuzzy.

In the mid-1980s, by contrast, a property was easier to classify. With some exceptions, a film property was a film property, and merchandise based on it sold for a relatively short window—about six to eight weeks on average. Similarly, a property that relied upon television as its primary media vehicle—*The Smurfs*, for example—remained mainly television-based. Merchandising activity continued as long as the show was on the air, and then pretty much ended.

Starting in the late 1980s and early 1990s, however, television began to be perceived as one part of the overall entertainment and marketing plan for a licensed property. In the early 1990s, manufacturers and retailers were in the midst of a stubborn recession, and wanted to minimize the risk inherent in most licensed entertainment properties. As a result, the licensor's plans for extending a property throughout various entertainment media was considered a key selling point for manufacturers choosing a license, and for retailers making purchase decisions about licensed merchandise. And, although the industry is emerging from the recession in the mid-1990s, the conservative attitude toward choosing properties remains.

The strategy of expanding across media minimizes risk in part because it keeps the property fresh over a longer period. Each new entertainment vehicle provides additional opportunities to promote licensed merchandise as well as offering new graphics and new themes on which merchandise can be based. It also lessens a property's reliance on any one media element to guarantee success. For example, if a television show is canceled, the property can still be kept alive in the form of films, sequels, video-game releases, comics, book publishing, home video releases of films and television episodes, and so on.

Many of today's most successful television-related licensed properties have this multimedia outlook in common. *Star Trek*, for example, has exceeded $2 billion in total retail sales, according to licensor Viacom Consumer Products. The property has generated four television series, with a fifth to launch in 1995, each with a different cast (except for the animated 1960s version, which was based on Captain Kirk and the rest of the original live-action cast). Seven films have been released as of the end of 1994. Video and computer game releases for Sega, Nintendo, and various other hardware platforms; video releases of all the films and several of the television episodes; and an extensive publishing series, with many of the books on bestseller lists, all contribute to *Star Trek*'s longevity and ever-increasing sales of licensed products.

Another good example is the Batman franchise. Three live-action films and an animated one have driven sales since 1989. The animated series airing on Fox, various home video releases, publishing, and video games all contribute to the property's success, as do the DC Comics comic books (in which Batman originated) and the 1960s television series starring Adam West, which can still be seen in reruns. Retail sales of licensed merchandise worldwide approach $2 billion to date, according to Warner Bros. Consumer Products, the property's licensor.

Walt Disney's *The Little Mermaid* was launched as an animated film, which should be re-released every seven years or so, as per Disney's usual strategy. While sales of merchandise have fallen off, home video series, an animated series, an extensive publishing program, and audio recordings all keep the property alive. These media vehicles, significantly, will allow merchandising potential to continue into the future—and as new generations of children are born, the franchise can be reintroduced to each one. Retail sales of Little Mermaid merchandise reached about the $1 billion mark in 1989–90, according to Walt Disney Consumer Products.

Finally, the Teenage Mutant Ninja Turtles, recent licensing stars with over $4 billion in retail sales of licensed merchandise worldwide, have been the focus of three films with at least a fourth and probably several more planned through a recent agreement with New Line Cinema. The television series (which began in 1987 and still airs on CBS as of this writing), various home videos of both the television series and films, a best-selling video-game series, and an active program of both book publishing and comic books (where, of course, the Turtles began) all contribute to the property's longevity.

The list goes on. All of these licensing efforts, with their variety of media exposure—including but not limited to television—create and maintain customer awareness, provide continuing opportunities for promotions, and constantly make new characters and designs available for licensing. Even relatively new properties are embarking on the same journey. The licensors of the Power Rangers and Barney, for example, both have plans for feature film releases within the next few years, both have live mall tours or stage shows, and both properties are active in publishing, star in electronic games, and the like. All of this activity springs from the licensors'—and licensees' and retailers'—desire for a long property life span.

While each of these new entertainment vehicles extends and strengthens the overall franchise, it should be noted that each new venue is usually treated by licensors as a separate property. Thus each requires separate contract negotiations, and sometimes ends up with a somewhat different licensee list (although the bulk of licensees usually sign on for all or most of the properties within the franchise). In some cases, competing licensees may become involved with the same franchise, each associated with a different entertainment vehicle.

Consolidation within the Entertainment Business

Consolidation within the entertainment business is an ongoing trend that, like those discussed so far, promises to have a big impact on television licensing. Entertainment conglomerates are looking to increase intra-company synergies, hoping to maximize profitability. At the same time, many large entertainment companies are hoping to enter new, related areas where they do not yet do business. The so-called "information superhighway," no matter what form it takes or when it finally arrives, is encouraging many entertainment companies to position themselves as providers of both hardware—distribution channels as well as proprietary technologies—and, especially, software in the form of programming.

Consolidation is one way for an entertainment provider to control as many aspects of its business as possible and to fully leverage its assets within the structure of the company. For example, owning a terrestrial or cable network, or a syndication arm, allows a film studio to control distribution of its intellectual property. Owning production subsidiaries allows intellectual property to be internally developed and fully owned, as opposed to being acquired from third parties. Launching publishing companies, home video

arms, and even manufacturing facilities allows entertainment entities to better control ancillary marketing of their intellectual properties. And, operating retail stores allows more control over how
consumer products based on a company's own properties are distributed and merchandised.

A long list of examples illustrates the existence of this trend.
The Walt Disney company produces and distributes television programming and films; it owns a cable network, the Disney Channel;
it controls publishing through four in-house imprints; it distributes
home videos and audio recordings of its own and other content
providers; it markets its own interactive games; and it owns retail
stores and theme parks. The Turner organization owns several
cable networks, film archives, and studios including, recently, New
Line Cinema and Castle Rock; it has its own publishing and home
video arms; and it owns Hanna-Barbera, the animation production
house.

Similarly, Warner Bros. distributes films and television vehicles, and produces television programming; it owns magazine
and book publishing operations; it operates a successful retail chain
and owns theme parks; and it distributes home video and audio
products. Sony is involved in film distribution, television production and distribution, apparel manufacturing and music merchandising, audio recordings, video games and multimedia products,
electronics, and so on. And Viacom, with its recent purchase of
Paramount, now owns a film studio, several cable networks, a
group of theme parks, a major publishing house, an interactive
game division, a television distribution and production arm, and
so forth.

While the above examples focus mainly on huge Hollywood
conglomerates, other companies also have several different businesses under their corporate umbrellas. Hearst, Spelling Entertainment, and New World Entertainment are all examples of this trend.
Each either owns or has associations with several companies in
various facets of the entertainment business.

How does this consolidation within the entertainment industry
affect television merchandising? First, most of the companies enumerated above have active licensing divisions to control the merchandising of all the intellectual property assets created or
managed throughout the company's various divisions. This situation means not only that the licensing division offers its expertise to
properties culled from all branches of the conglomerate, but also

that all of a company's assets are centrally scrutinized for their licensing potential and for possible synergies with other company-owned properties or distribution channels. In addition, it allows properties from all subsidiaries to be re-created in new entertainment forms by other divisions in the company. If each of the subsidiaries or divisions of a company were separately owned, some of the assets would be mined, others would not; but in this way, licensing becomes recognized as a major profit center.

For example, the Hanna-Barbera library contains a classic character, Space Ghost, among its thousands of properties. Space Ghost was dormant for many years, but fairly soon after the purchase of Hanna-Barbera by the Turner organization, the character developed into a good example of synergy. Space Ghost is the focus of a series developed by Turner called *Space Ghost: Coast to Coast*, airing on Turner's Cartoon Network. Turner's licensing and merchandising division is looking into the licensing potential for the character, and other of the company's divisions may become involved with Space Ghost as well.

Consolidation also affects licensing by encouraging intra-company merchandising deals. Licensing personnel first seek out ways in which other branches of the same company can benefit from a property, before they seek outside licensees. For example, Sony Signatures, a division of entertainment conglomerate Sony, has the capability to make T-shirts and other apparel, as well as interactive games, audio and video recordings, television shows, and films. Two of its divisions, Sony Signatures Retail Distribution and Sony Electronic Publishing, are often among the first licensees signed to make T-shirts and electronic games, respectively, based on properties controlled by Sony Signatures Licensing. Sony's television properties include *The Critic*, *Days of Our Lives*, and *Beakman's World*, among others.

Finally, consolidation means that these entertainment companies, which are traditionally licensors, are now increasingly acting as licensees as well. The organizations are not only looking to maximize opportunities for their own properties through their ownership of publishing arms, home video arms, apparel manufacturing facilities, and the like, but they are also seeking third-party properties with which they might associate as licensees. Many of these licensors have been licensees in the entertainment field for some time, of course, making films, television series, or audio and video recordings based on outside properties. Now, however, they are capable of becoming publishing, video-game, or T-shirt licensees as well. For example, Sony Signatures Retail is an apparel licensee for many non-Sony properties, including Spelling's *Melrose Place*.

The expansion of these major entertainment powerhouses into new product categories and non-traditional businesses, of course, means that they become even more formidable competitors for smaller, independent licensors of television properties. And, they are also competing with smaller licensees in the product categories that they are newly entering.

Increasing Consumer Sophistication about Licensing

Another important trend in television licensing and licensing generally is an increasing sophistication on the part of consumers. The availability of licensed merchandise has proliferated over the last decade, and consumers have become very discriminating about what licensed products they choose to buy. Fifteen years ago, the fact that a product exhibited a licensed property in itself made that product somewhat a novelty, and therefore attractive to consumers. Now, however, so much licensed merchandise based on television and other entertainment properties is available in the marketplace that being licensed alone does not make a product unique.

Consumers are still attracted to licensed merchandise based on properties they like, but now the merchandise itself must also be something they are willing to buy. It is not enough just to imprint the likeness of a character or logo on a T-shirt, put it on a store shelf, and assume it will sell. The product itself must—with a few exceptions—be perceived as having value for the dollar, and must incorporate fashion trends, play value, or other attributes that make generic, nonlicensed products in the same category sell.

This trend means that more merchandise finds its way into upscale distribution channels such as department and specialty stores, and carries higher price points than it has in the past, as well. While the mass market still accounts for a large percentage of licensed entertainment and character merchandise sales, other distribution channels are increasingly viewed as viable. In addition, manufacturers in product categories in which licensing was never really a big factor—ranging from prepaid telephone calling cards to computer screensavers—are now amenable to considering licensed properties.

All of this is significant because it means that licensors must increasingly work in partnership with their licensees and with retailers to develop products that will sell. The licensed property itself, whether a television show or other entertainment property, is still an incentive to encourage consumers to purchase an item, and is attractive to manufacturers as a way to differentiate their brands. But, increasingly, the products themselves must also meet the high standards of consumers; they must be items that consumers would consider buying regardless of whether they incorporate the image of their favorite television series. For a licensed product line to be successful, consumers must feel both an affinity for the television show and a respect for the product's quality and value; both contribute importantly to the final purchase decision.

*   *   *

Because of all of the trends outlined in this chapter, television licensing is becoming increasingly complex. More participants are getting involved in licensing in various ways as a result of these developments. Simultaneously, more licensing partners are often included in the merchandising activities of single properties, in turn multiplying the complexity level. Chapter 3 will sort out in more detail who the various players are, summarize their roles and responsibilities, and discuss how these factors are evolving as a result of the changes outlined here.

Chapter 3
Who Are the Players?

As noted throughout this book, television productions and the licensing agreements that spring from them are becoming more complex as costs go up and more players become involved. On the licensor side alone, the more partners involved in a production, the more difficult it is to divide the rights, responsibilities, and rewards among them.

In addition to the fact that more participants have a hand in production and often in the licensing effort surrounding a television show, those players are also increasingly diverse. The fact that television productions are being financed more creatively means that companies who may not have been involved in entertainment are now entering the fray. Often these organizations are licensors from other areas (such as publishing or electronic game firms, which allow their characters to star in a television vehicle). They may have previously licensed their properties to entertainment companies, of course, but now they are increasingly involved in the financing of the productions, and are sometimes setting up joint ventures and subsidiaries for the purpose of creating entertainment vehicles based on their intellectual properties.

The comic book industry is a good example of this trend. In 1992, Malibu Graphics merged with video-game publisher Acme Interactive to form Malibu Comics Entertainment (purchased by Marvel Comics at the end of 1994), while in the same year Dark Horse Comics and interactive multimedia developer Total Vision formed Dark Vision Interactive to market interactive multimedia titles based on theatrical films and comic book characters. Meanwhile, these two comics publishers, among many others, are more actively involved in television and film productions based on their properties. Dark Horse, for example, was the source of the animated series *Duckman* on the USA Network.

Within the entertainment industry, as the big Hollywood conglomerates grow and diversify into related businesses, licensing and/or production partnerships increasingly involve multiple sister companies under the same corporate umbrella. One or more of the divisions may act as property owners while others assume the role of licensees. For example, sister companies acting as licensor/partners include Turner Licensing & Merchandising representing Turner unit CNN's logo for merchandising; licensing agent Hamilton Projects handling parent company Spelling Entertainment's productions, such as *Melrose Place* and *Models, Inc.;* and Warner Bros., which creates entertainment based on, and acts as licensing agent for, properties from Time-Warner's DC Comics division, including Batman and many others.

Meanwhile, intra-company licensing arrangements include *Mary Shelley's Frankenstein*, a film handled by Sony Signatures Licensing, for which apparel is manufactured by Sony Signatures Retail; *Pagemaster*, an animated movie distributed in the United States by Fox, who also represents it for licensing, which is authorized to Fox Interactive for CD-ROM games; and *Star Trek*, a Paramount property licensed by sister company Viacom Consumer Products, among whose licensees is a third Viacom unit, Simon & Schuster.

Another development contributing to the complexity of television licensing is the increasingly global nature of television production and licensing. This trend, which will be discussed in more detail in Chapter 6, means that not only are there more players, but they represent varied tastes, cultures, and ways of doing business. And, they are geographically far removed, which makes partnerships logistically more difficult.

The increasingly complicated nature of agreements among property owners can be illustrated with a few examples of television properties that, as of this writing, have licensing programs in the United States. *The Adventures of Dudley the Dragon*, for example, a Canadian show now being aired on public television stations in the United States (with American Program Services as its distributor) is produced by Breakthrough Films & Television in association with TV Ontario/LaChaine Francais, with the participation of Telefilm Canada, Rogers Telefund, and the Ontario Film Investment Program. Meridian Direct has been retained as the program's licensing agent.

Similarly, *Mighty Max*, an animated children's series based on a British toy, is a collaboration between Bluebird Toy, the property owner; Canal+, the French television company; and animator Film Roman. Mattel as the U.S. master toy licensee and distributor Bohbot Entertainment are also involved. Leisure Concepts is the property's licensing agent in the United States.

Finally, *ReBoot*, a Saturday morning series featuring computer-generated graphics, is a co-production of Alliance Communications and BLT Productions, in association with U.S. network ABC, Canadian network YTV, and Meridien. Licensing agent Total Licensing Services handles merchandising. Such complicated ownership and financing structures lead to a number of questions as to how licensing responsibilities and rewards should be divided and by whom the licensing program should be administered.

The Major Players

The diverse entities involved in television licensing can be divided into a number of categories, at least for descriptive purposes. Many of these types of companies have been discussed earlier during the examination of trends, but they will be briefly summarized here in order to provide an orderly overview of the whole television licensing world.

Hollywood studios

The major Hollywood studios are active players not only in television production, but also in licensing. Warner Brothers, Viacom Consumer Products (associated with Paramount Pictures), Walt Disney, Twentieth Century Fox, MCA/Universal (owner of Universal Pictures), and Sony (owner of TriStar and Columbia), for example, are all involved in television production and distribution (Figure 3.1). All of them have active licensing departments.

Increasing synergies between sister companies, mentioned earlier, is as evident with the studios as with any other group of licensors. For example, the studios' licensing divisions look for

FIGURE 3.1   The *Beakman's World*™ licensing program is handled by Sony Signatures, a Hollywood company with film and television production and distribution capabilities, as well as the ability to create interactive software and apparel, among other businesses.

properties to represent from within all arms of their sister organizations. Properties from all company units are also exploited in various entertainment vehicles produced within the organization, if opportunities exist. Most of the studios have the capability—through sister companies or subsidiaries—to create publishing, interactive games, video and audio releases, theme parks, and live events.

For example, entertainment company MCA is involved with two video-game characters, Boogerman and Clay Fighter, owned by electronic game manufacturer Interplay, of which MCA purchased a significant minority share in 1994 and is the company's sole outside investor. MCA Television is developing the two properties for children's animated series scheduled for 1995, while the studio's licensing division, MCA/Universal Merchandising, handles merchandising.

Other studios that manage licensing departments or are involved in licensing include MGM, Orion, and New Line (now owned by Turner).

Other multimedia conglomerates

Companies outside of the major Hollywood studios are exhibiting many similar trends. They own or have relationships with companies involved in film and television production and distribution, and maintain interests in publishing, electronic games, audio, and home video. Like the studios, they consider licensing and merchandising to be a major profit center, and seek properties from throughout their divisions.

The Hearst organization is one example. It is involved in television production and distribution through Hearst Broadcasting Productions, Hearst Entertainment Distribution, and Hearst Entertainment Productions. It owns interests in several cable networks, including Arts & Entertainment, Lifetime, ESPN, and New England Cable News. In publishing, it owns a book publisher (William Morrow), fourteen magazines, and twelve newspapers, as well as being involved in four electronic publishing ventures. It owns three newspaper syndication operations, as well, including Cowles Syndicate, King Features Syndicate, and North America Syndicate. As for licensing, its King Features Licensing division handles comic strip and entertainment properties including Popeye, Betty Boop, and the Berenstain Bears. Hearst Magazines is also separately involved in licensing for its published titles, especially *Cosmopolitan*, *Popular Mechanics*, and *Sports Afield*.

Another instance is Turner Broadcasting System, which owns the Hanna-Barbera animation studio; Turner Publishing, including the imprint Bedrock Press; a library of classic films from MGM,

RKO, and others; film studios; interactive game capabilities; cable networks, including the Cartoon Network and CNN; and television production and distribution arms.

Similarly, the MacAndrews & Forbes investment company, run by financier Ron Perelman, owns Marvel Entertainment, which markets comic books, trading cards, and toys (the latter two through subsidiaries); New World Entertainment, a production house; portions of a television station ownership group; and syndicator Genesis Entertainment. Increasing signs of cooperation are beginning to appear among the various units of this organization; for example, syndicated television shows involving New World and Genesis are based on Marvel Comics characters, with licensed toys and trading cards by Marvel subsidiaries Toy Biz and Fleer, respectively.

Viacom is also an example, now owning Paramount Pictures; Nickelodeon, MTV, and other cable networks; television distribution arms; and publisher Simon & Schuster. Since licensing activities are not centralized at this writing, however, Paramount, MTV, and Nickelodeon are covered in their respective categories (Hollywood studios and broadcast and cable networks) for the purposes of this discussion.

Broadcast and cable networks

While most networks' participation in licensing is less than that of the Hollywood studios or the other multimedia entertainment companies discussed so far, they are involved, and should become more so. In broadcast, for example, ABC and CBS both hired dedicated licensing personnel in 1994, and NBC also has several properties available for merchandising. The new Warner and United/Paramount networks' licensing activity—which is likely—will be handled by the parent companies' licensing divisions.

Similarly, the Fox network's significant merchandising activity is handled by Fox's licensing arm, mentioned in the section on Hollywood studios. Fox has, as of this writing, been the most active broadcast network in taking ownership positions in the shows it airs. It owns the copyrights to *The Tick* and *Eek the Cat*, for example, among others. According to *Entertainment Law & Finance*, an industry newsletter, Fox controls more than 50% of the licensing rights for shows it owns, and has between 5% and 15% participation in merchandising for programs it airs but does not own.

While some broadcast networks and syndicators (see below) still prefer upfront advertising dollars (clearances) as their full payment for handling or broadcasting a show, Fox's activity is indicative of the fact that a growing number of these companies are seeking participation in merchandising as part of the financial package.

Finally, the Public Broadcasting System is also involved in licensing by virtue of its investment in some of its programming, which it is increasingly looking to recoup through a percentage of merchandising revenues. In addition, PBS has begun licensing its proprietary characters, the P-Pals.

Many cable networks also have licensing departments, or personnel with licensing as part of their jurisdiction. Nickelodeon and MTV—which, as noted, are both part of the Viacom family—are among the most active examples. ESPN and HBO also are involved in licensing, as are the Cartoon Network, CNN, and USA to some extent (with licensing activities handled by sister companies Turner for the Cartoon Network and CNN, and Viacom for USA). Many other cable networks are looking into licensing, as well, although to date their activity has not been significant.

Independent production and distribution companies

Independent production companies and television distributors (including organizations with capability for both) are beginning to increase their presence in the licensing business. Although many have been involved to some extent, more are now actively seeking to reap the benefits of licensing in generating both awareness and ancillary income, either in-house or with the help of licensing agents. They are also looking to maximize their share of merchandising revenues generated by their programs, even if another company (such as a studio) is the primary force behind the licensing program.

Just a few examples of the independent production and distribution companies with licensing departments include Saban Entertainment, handling *Mighty Morphin Power Rangers*, *V.R. Troopers*, *Creepy Crawlers*, and *Sweet Valley High*, among other properties; DIC Entertainment, with *Rimba's Island*, *Superhuman Samurai Syber-Squad*, and others; Bohbot, a relatively new player, with *Double Dragon* and *Highlander*; Nelvana, with *Babar* and *Tales From The*

Crypt, among others; ITC Entertainment, with classic series such as *Thunderbirds* that are being reintroduced to today's children; and Zodiac Entertainment, which produces *Widget, Mr. Bogus*, and *Twinkle, the Dream Being*, and licenses them out in conjunction with its agent Camelot Licensing.

Independent stations

Some independent stations are involved in production or co-production of television shows, and as a result are becoming more interested in licensing. Many are public television stations. For example, KCET-Los Angeles, a partner in the production of PBS show *The Puzzle Place*, has a staff member for whom licensing is one major responsibility, and WGBH-Boston recently announced its intention to get more involved in merchandising its programs, which include *NOVA* and *This Old House*. Similarly, WQED-Pittsburgh is a partner in the U.S. production of *Johnson & Friends*, an Australian pre-school program that was launched in the United States on the Fox Children's Network in fall 1994. (Fox is the lead licensor for the U.S. market.)

Outside licensors

Property owners from outside the television business are a significant—and growing—part of the mix. Their properties are often developed into television shows, and in many cases they help to finance those programs. As the original property owner, they share in merchandising revenues and—since they frequently have prior experience as licensors and are set up for licensing—they often administer the merchandising programs for the television shows, as well. Comics publisher Marvel, for example, handles licensing for *X-Men*, produced by Saban and aired on Fox, which is based on a Marvel comic book.

In addition, several non-entertainment licensors are partially owned by entertainment companies. For example, Harvey Entertainment, the licensor of the Harvey Comics characters, including Casper the Friendly Ghost, Richie Rich, and many others, all of which are being examined for exploitation in films and television— Casper and Richie star in films in 1994 and 1995—is 10.6% owned by MCA, parent company of Universal Pictures. Interestingly, Harvey recently stopped publishing comic books in-house, licensing those rights to Marvel. It has now become a full-time licensor of its many properties.

Probably the most prolific types of outside licensors, as measured by the number of properties that ultimately become television shows, are comic book publishers, electronic game manufacturers (both video and computer games), book publishers, and toy marketers. For example, comic book properties that made the jump to television programs include Mirage Comics' *Teenage Mutant Ninja Turtles*; DC Comics' *Batman*; *Tales from the Crypt*, which was originally a comic property of E.C. Comics; Dark Horse Comics' *The Mask*; and Marvel's *Iron Man*, *Fantastic Four*, *Spiderman*, and *X-Men*. Most comic book companies have licensing staff on board. (Newspaper comic strips also find their way into television series and specials, including *Beakman's World*, handled for licensing by Sony Signatures, and *Peanuts*, handled by United Media.)

Another area that gives birth to a large number of properties is the realm of video and computer games. Sega's Sonic the Hedgehog, Broderbund's Carmen Sandiego, which was the inspiration for two television shows (a live-action game show on public television and an animated series on Fox), Nintendo's Super Mario Bros., Capcom's Mega Man, and Electronic Arts' Mutant League all originated as consumer electronics-based properties and have all developed into television or other entertainment vehicles.

Book properties that have made their way to television include Babar, which is jointly licensed by Nelvana and the Clifford Ross Company; *The Magic School Bus*, owned by Scholastic; *The Busy World of Richard Scarry*, handled by Viacom Consumer Products; Beatrix Potter's works, starring Peter Rabbit and friends, licensed by the Copyrights Group; and *Madeline*, handled by DIC Entertainment. The merchandising rights to these properties often lie with the author or his or her estate, rather than with the publishing company. Some publishers, however, are active in licensing and either own properties or represent authors in their merchandising efforts. Scholastic Productions, which is also involved in various other entertainment media, such as home video and television production, in addition to publishing, is one example.

Toy companies are also active as outside licensors, although they were stronger as a source of properties in the 1980s than they are in the 1990s. Television shows—past and present—based on toys include Mattel's *He-Man and the Masters of the Universe*,

Hasbro's *My Little Pony* and *Transformers Generation II*, and Blue-bird Toys' *Mighty Max*.

Actors, writers, and others in the creative community

While actors, writers, directors, musicians, stunt personnel, and their agents and unions are rarely involved in licensing from an administrative standpoint, they are sometimes involved as rights owners. Many actors, especially those in starring roles, retain approval rights over the use of their likenesses, and may also share in merchandising revenues. In some cases, the star of a show is involved more heavily in its production, contributing financially, sharing in producing chores, or creating the concept on which the show is based. In such cases the actor's involvement in licensing will usually be greater, both in terms of the share of merchandising income and in regard to administering the licensing program; he or she may approve products, for example.

One example is William Shatner's *Tek,* based on a series of science fiction novels he wrote. Shatner's company licensed Marvel for comics and Cardz Distribution for trading cards. Ultimately the property was developed into a series of live-action made-for-television films syndicated as part of MCA Television's *Action Pack* syndication package. MCA/Universal Merchandising took over licensing responsibilities for products based on the television version.

Even when the talent does not have a financial or creative stake in the production, licensors need to obtain clearances to use actors' likenesses on products (Figure 3.2). For live-action television programs, the ability to provide artwork portraying the show's characters is very important, for two reasons. First, consumer demand for products incorporating the actors is generally greater than demand for items sporting only the show's logo. Secondly, having a large library of artwork or photographs available from which licensees can select allows them more flexibility in creating products, providing more variety in their merchandise mix. The latter ability is important because it gives customers more products from which to choose, increasing the likelihood that they will want to own something. A wide variety of merchandise can also encourage customers to buy more than one item, either simultaneously or over a period of time.

FIGURE 3.2 Licensors of shows starring live, recognizable actors, such as *X-Files*, with David Duchovny and Gillian Anderson, must usually get clearances from talent before authorizing their depictions to be incorporated into licensed products.

The X-Files ™ and © 1995 Twentieth Century Fox Film Corporation. All Rights Reserved. Used by Permission. Photo Credit: Michael Grecco/Fox.

The agent for the *Beverly Hills 90210* licensing effort, for example, acquired clearances for a library of 100 photographs of the actors in the series, which licensees could use in addition to the show's logo. All American's *Baywatch* and Paramount Television's

Star Trek are other examples of programs where actors' likenesses are essential to the licensing program.

Licensing agents

Licensing agents are hired by property owners to represent their interests in launching and administering a merchandising effort. Some licensors retain one agent to handle all of their properties, others hire a separate agent for each property in their stable, while others forego an agent altogether, preferring to handle merchandising in-house. For a multi-partner television production, an agent who has an existing relationship with one of the partners may administer the licensing effort for the show. Conversely, a licensing agent from outside the partnership may be retained to handle merchandising.

On occasion, a licensing agent may have a financial stake in the production of a television show, or may be a partial owner of the underlying property on which the show is based. In that case, the agent is one of the partners, rather than simply a licensing agent in the traditional sense. The agency may not be remunerated with a straight commission of licensing revenues, as most agents are, but may rather receive a percentage of profits based on its share of equity ownership.

Licensing agents can also be actively involved in the production of a television series. For example, the animated series *Mega Man*, which is being produced by Ruby-Spears, counts as its executive producer the president of Entertainment Licensing Associates. ELA is the licensing agent for Capcom, a video-game company that owns the character Mega Man, on which the syndicated show is based.

Licensees

While licensees are not traditionally a party in the ownership of a television program—they lease the rights to a property for incorporation into their merchandise, but do not share in ownership—there are cases when they do participate more fully. They may financially back a television show based on a property for which they are a licensee, if they feel that their participation in the production is a worthwhile investment. The added awareness the show brings to the licensee's products may increase sales, in which case the investment in the show is analogous to an advertising expenditure. Some manufacturers also have expertise as licensors as well as licensees, and thus may be best qualified to take over the day-to-day administration of a television-based licensing effort with which they are involved.

Toy companies are probably the best example of this participation. Since toy sales can account for from one-third to two-thirds of total retail sales of licensed merchandise based on a children's entertainment property, and because their investment in the property is high—in product development, retooling, and advertising costs, for example—they already have a significant financial interest in the properties with which they associate. Thus they may want to protect their stake by taking a more active role in the television production.

This involvement is distinguished from the examples cited above under "Outside licensors," where a toy company owns the rights to a property and acts primarily as a licensor, granting the rights for a television production as well as for other merchandise based on the property. In this case, the toy manufacturer is a licensee that acquires the rights from the licensor, whether it be a comic book company, publisher, or entertainment company. As a licensee with a great stake in the property, the toy company may then decide to offer money for the production of the television program, or may handle the licensing program for the television producer or other licensor.

One example of such a situation is *The Teenage Mutant Ninja Turtles* (Figure 3.3). Mirage Comics is the licensor of the original property, Surge Entertainment is the licensing agent, and Playmates is the master toy licensee. In 1988, Playmates financed the first five episodes of the syndicated Turtles animated series. It recouped its investment through increased sales of its own toy line, as well as through a share of royalties from other licensees who made products based on the series.

Other parties

Any company or person who has a financial interest in a television show or in a property on which a television show is based may be involved in the licensing effort in some way, whether assuming an active day-to-day role or simply receiving a percentage of royalty revenues. For example, various financial institutions could hold a

FIGURE 3.3   Playmates, the master toy licensee for *The Teenage Mutant Ninja Turtles*, helped finance the initial episodes of the animated television series. Pictured here (from left), Michaelangelo, Leonardo, Raphael, and (front) Donatello.

© Mirage Studios, exclusively licensed by Surge Licensing, Inc.

financial stake in a program, but their expertise in licensing may be limited. While they may receive a percentage of merchandising revenues, their role in day-to-day operations will most likely be negligible.

An example of a corporation outside the entertainment industry with a financial interest in a television-based licensing program is the fashion label Guess. Guess is involved in a joint venture with DIC Entertainment for an entertainment concept called "Wild Guess," for which some of the proceeds from licensing go to the Wild Guess Foundation, a non-profit environmental organization set up in conjunction with the venture. The concept subsequently developed into a television show called *Rimba's Island*, which is available for licensing and has signed deals for apparel, accessories, bed and bath, toys, school supplies, publishing, party goods, plush, and more. DIC is the lead licensor, but Guess is involved as well. (Incidentally, Guess is a licensor in its own right in the fashion industry, authorizing other companies to make apparel and accessories under the Guess label.)

Rights, Responsibilities, and Rewards

The relative participation of the groups of players outlined above varies. The division of rights, responsibilities, and rewards covers a variety of distinct categories, including ownership of intellectual property rights, division of financial inputs and incoming revenues, control of licensing strategies and day-to-day administration, and product approvals.

Ownership of intellectual property

Intellectual property rights include ownership of trademarks and copyrights, as well as, in some cases, patents. Trademarks and copyrights are the major areas of concern for television-based licensing programs, however. As will be noted in more detail in Chapter 4, trademarks and copyrights are both methods of legally protecting a property, barring others from infringing upon it. Adequate copyright and trademark protection provides value to licensees, which can use a legally protected property to differentiate their merchandise from that of their competitors.

Copyrights involve the creative elements of the television production, including art, music, and text. Trademarks, on the other hand, apply to names, depictions, and logos that distinguish the goods and services of one company from those of another. Trademarks, therefore, are the primary method of protecting properties for licensing purposes, although copyright is also used.

Divvying up the ownership of intellectual property is fairly straightforward in many cases. For example, if a production company creates a television show and handles licensing in-house, or retains a licensing agent on a straight commission, it will register the appropriate trademarks and copyrights and retain full ownership. When several partners are involved in the creation of a television show, on the other hand, the ownership of rights to various trademarks and copyrights may be a matter for negotiation. Similarly, if a series is based on an existing property and incorporates elements of the original along with newly created, television-specific elements, the issue of intellectual property ownership can become more complicated.

For example, for *Bobby's World*, an animated series on the Fox Children's Network, the Bobby character is trademarked in the name of Alevy Productions, while Fox Children's Network holds the copyrights and trademarks for the remaining elements of the show. Similarly, the animated series *Superhuman Samurai Syber-Squad*, distributed by All American, is a new show based on a Japanese character named Power Boy (which is a spin-off of the classic Ultraman film and television series). DIC Entertainment is the producer, in association with Tsuburaya Productions, the Japanese licensor of Power Boy and Ultraman. New elements of the program are copyrighted by DIC Entertainment, while Tsuburaya holds the copyrights for the original elements.

Finally, Fred Wolf Films' *Teenage Mutant Ninja Turtles* animated series is based on a Mirage Comics publication. Mirage holds the copyrights to the original comic book, and also owns the trademarks for the Turtles. Meanwhile, Fred Wolf Films holds the copyrights for the animated series.

Administration of the licensing program

The responsibility for overseeing the licensing program must also be assigned to one or more parties involved in the television production. This broad area—overseeing the program—can be broken down into three smaller segments: developing a licensing strategy, day-to-day administration of the licensing program, and quality control.

Developing a licensing strategy involves creating an overall plan for most effectively launching the effort, so as to maximize either revenue generation, awareness, or both. It also involves keeping the property fresh throughout its life span by virtue of new entertainment vehicles and promotional activities. Developing a strategy requires a knowledge of the characteristics of the property itself and of its target audience, and an awareness of how to best market and sell licensed products while maintaining the integrity of the property.

The second aspect of the licensing program, its day-to-day administration, involves implementing the strategies discussed above, keeping in touch with licensees and retailers, looking for and signing licensees and products that are appropriate for the property throughout its life, and instituting promotions. Administering a licensing program requires that a staff be in place to handle these duties. It also necessitates a specific knowledge of how retailers operate and of the manufacturing process in various categories. It is also beneficial to have contacts within the licensing and retail communities, as well as expertise in the mechanics of licensing.

The third facet of licensing responsibility is quality control. It encompasses two main areas, licensee selection and product approval processes. Both are primarily part of the day-to-day administration of the licensing effort, and are thus handled by the partner with responsibility in this area. Because product approvals are such an important aspect of maintaining the integrity of the property itself, however, other partners, especially the trademark and copyright owner or owners, may be involved.

In general, the partner with the greatest expertise in licensing is best equipped to take responsibility for all three facets of licensing administration. If one partner has a knowledgeable and experienced staff in place, has contacts within the consumer product and retail communities, and knows the ropes as far as promotional support, that partner is likely to be best qualified to assume control of this aspect of the licensing effort. If no partners have the requisite expertise, a licensing agent is usually retained, who can provide the expertise in return for a commission of licensing revenues. This percentage is taken off the top, before the remaining royalties, advances, and guarantees are divided among the other players.

Sometimes the division of responsibilities can be complicated. For example, if all the parties have expertise and all are involved financially in the production, other factors will come into play when making the decision about who should handle licensing. A venture that includes a major studio and a large outside licensor and a production company with licensing experience, for example, would bring three experienced parties to the table. Such an arrangement would also feature three partners who prefer at least partial control over licensing, not just in terms of earning a fair share of revenues, but also in decision making.

One example of an alliance involving several companies with licensing capability is *The Mask* animated series. It, along with the 1994 film of the same name, is based on a Dark Horse Comics character. The partners include Dark Horse, which owns the original property (and whose president also serves as executive producer of the television show), co-producers New Line (who also distributed the film) and Sunbow, and animator Film Roman. These partners all have some licensing experience and/or licensing personnel. New Line is the lead licensor for the television version, as it was for the film.

No matter how responsibilities are divided up behind the scenes, a united front should be presented to potential licensees and retailers, preferably with one of the partners or a licensing agent acting as their primary contact.

Financial rewards and responsibilities

Each television licensing situation is unique, and there is no standard method of dividing the monetary rewards. Since each agreement is subject to negotiation, the relative bargaining power of the players is one factor. A licensor with a new property who is dealing with a major television production company or studio will have less bargaining power than one with a well-established property negotiating with a smaller or less experienced production company.

The relative amount of financial resources put into the production by each partner is also a factor in the decision about how to divide royalty revenues. The more financing a given partner provides, the more its share of licensing revenue is likely to be. Likewise, when a network helps with financing—or sometimes simply in exchange for the exposure it gives to the show—it will generally want some cut of merchandising revenues. For example, PBS invests significant funds up front, often in the $1 million to $2 million range, for the production of children's programming. It increasingly expects a cut of licensing royalties in return.

Similarly, according to reports in *Advertising Age*, the Fox Children's Network expects to receive "millions" as its portion of merchandising revenues from *Mighty Morphin Power Rangers*. This amount is just a drop in the bucket compared to the total flood of Power Rangers royalties that are expected to be generated over the life of the property; retail sales of Power Ranger merchandise surpassed $1 billion by 1995, according to industry observers. The vast majority of the royalties associated with these sales will go to Saban Entertainment, since it produces, distributes, and owns the show. Still, Fox will receive a share of this bounty (probably somewhere between 5% and 15% of royalties).

The amount of time and effort expended by each partner on a daily basis to implement the licensing program also affects the division of revenues. While licensing agents traditionally get a commission of 25% to 40% of royalty income on average, if they make a financial contribution they will probably negotiate a different type of deal, as noted earlier.

Summary of Considerations

It is difficult to lay out a typical arrangement showing how all of the different types of rewards, responsibilities, and rights are divided in an "average" television production, because each situation varies depending on who the partners are, their relative levels of expertise, their individual shares of the financial investment, their creative inputs, and their human resource and time commitment.

It is also difficult to find examples of how such deals are arranged, since most partners are privately held, and even if public, understandably do not give out information on how their behind-the-scenes deals are cut. One example that can be examined, however, due to the fact that it has been outlined in published reports in the *New York Times* and elsewhere, is the case of *The Puzzle Place*, a show set for launch on PBS affiliates beginning in 1995.

The players are Lancit Media, an independent production company, and KCET, the public television station in Los Angeles. The series is a co-production between these two entities. The Corporation for Public Broadcasting provided a $4.5 million grant in initial funding, while an additional $3.5 million for the first year's production came from Southern California Edison and Rebuild L.A., both of whom wanted to support the show's theme of multiculturalism. Licensing is handled by a 50%/50% joint venture between the Strategy Licensing Company, an 85%-owned subsidiary of Lancit Media that handles several outside properties in addition to Lancit's, and KCET.

The first three licensing deals alone reportedly brought in more than $5 million in guaranteed minimum royalties, $3.1 million from

Sony Wonder for audio and video recordings, $1.5 million from Fisher-Price for the master toy license, and $500,000 from Russ Berrie for gift items. More agreements have been signed as of this writing for products from footwear to party goods. In addition, it should be remembered that these are guaranteed minimum royalty payments; the actual royalties could easily surpass these amounts.

The joint venture licensing unit receives 40% of licensing royalties, which is within the normal range for a licensing agent's commission. The Corporation for Public Broadcasting receives 19%, unions representing people working on the show are due 11%, the creator of the puppets that star in the show earns 10%, and KCET and Lancit Media split the remaining 20%, according to a report in the *Times*.

This is a good illustration of a willingness to give up back-end revenues in return for upfront financing. Producers have traditionally eaten the deficit between production costs and license fees received from networks or stations, in the hopes of making their money on the back end from syndication, and to a lesser extent, merchandising. Now, however, producers are looking for upfront money to help finance the production and reduce their portion of the deficit; in return, the back-end revenues—of which an increasing share comes from merchandising, especially for children's shows—are split between the various parties who provide financing: studios, networks, or other partners.

In general, the negotiation process will ultimately determine who will be responsible for various inputs to the production—financial and otherwise—as well as for division of the economic rewards that will eventually accrue. Each partner must feel that what it is getting out of the television production and its licensing effort surpasses what it is putting in, and that its share is equitable to the shares of the other partners.

Chapter 4

Licensing Strategies and Their Implementation

Licensing programs vary depending upon the nature of the television show being licensed and its target audience, the resources and corporate strategy of the licensor, and the goals of the merchandising program. No two licensing efforts are exactly alike, although they often exhibit common characteristics.

Legally Protecting a Property

Since licensing is centered on the act of leasing a *legally protected* property, trademark and copyright registration is a prerequisite to any licensing program. Anyone planning to become involved in merchandising should retain an attorney who is well versed in intellectual property law, and more specifically, one with expertise in merchandise licensing. He or she should be consulted prior to taking any of the steps outlined here.

Trademarks are the primary legal protection upon which licensing is based. Names, slogans, graphic depictions, and other elements that distinguish one company's line of goods from those of a competitor can be trademarked through the Patent & Trademark Office (PTO) of the U.S. Department of Commerce. Since a television program will, through licensing, become an apparel brand, a toy brand, or a brand of stationery, appropriate trademark protection is essential. Trademarks must be registered in various classifications of goods, depending upon which product categories are planned.

Not only must trademarks be registered in the United States, they must also be registered in various countries where licensing is planned or where counterfeiting is likely to occur. Because all of this activity can become quite expensive, most licensing experts recommend a cost-benefit analysis with the help of an intellectual property attorney before proceeding. Trademark laws vary from country to country.

Copyright law offers a secondary method of legal protection. Copyright protects artwork, music, text, and logos, among other artistic or literary works, used in conjunction with products or in advertising or printed matter. They are registered through the Copyright Office of the U.S. Library of Congress.

While trademarks and copyrights are the primary legal tools used by licensors, other bodies of law may become relevant. For example, "trade dress"—the protectability of the overall look of a product or packaging—and the "right of publicity"—the right of a celebrity (or his or her heirs) to commercially exploit the name and image of that celebrity—may come into play in certain situations.

Creating a Licensing Strategy

Once a property is adequately protected through legal channels, it is time to develop a strategy for the licensing program.

Identifying objectives

Before embarking on a licensing effort, a property owner should examine and prioritize its goals. Is the major reason for the licensing effort to recoup the cost of producing the television series? If so, maximizing advance payments from licensees will probably be a key strategy. A licensing program based on this objective alone, however, will be unlikely to last for a long time; too much product out on the market at once increases the risk of oversaturation, which will cut a licensing effort short. On the other hand, if a licensor's goal is to increase awareness for a long-term brand such as a network logo, its strategy will be to create and manage a very slow-growing and controlled licensing program.

A third objective may be to create awareness for a brand-new television program. Toward this end, the licensor will want to make a strong statement by ensuring that a broad range of products is available at retail just prior to the show's premiere. In this case, the property owner might trade away high advances in order to convince a large number of manufacturers to take a chance on an unproven property. (It should be noted that, in most cases, merchandise that reaches retail too early will fail, because the television series is unknown. For a series based on an existing property such as a comic book, video game, book, or film, however, such a strategy may be viable.)

As is evident from these three examples, certain trade-offs exist, and the route taken depends on the licensor's objectives. A strategy for building awareness will differ from one for maximizing upfront money. No matter what the goals, however, maintaining the integrity of the property should be an important concern, particularly for a long-term property such as Nickelodeon, *Sesame Street*, Disney, or ABC Daytime.

Defining the property

In addition to setting objectives, a licensor must also thoroughly know its property. Important characteristics include the size and demographic characteristics of the property's target audience, its brand image (fun, educational, nostalgic), character attributes, storylines, and graphic look.

Competitive properties should also be analyzed. Often one licensee will have two or more "competing" entertainment properties in its line during the same season, so the idea of competition is somewhat different in licensing from its definition in other businesses. Still, a very strong-selling property will affect other properties targeted toward the same audience. For example, in 1993, other preschool properties felt the effects of Barney's strength; similarly, the power of the Power Rangers at its peak affected other boys' action properties, such as *Biker Mice From Mars*.

In general, the more thoroughly and concretely the property is defined and can be explained, the better a licensor will be able to sell it to manufacturers and retailers, and the better it will ultimately appeal to consumers.

Key Strategic Decisions

Within the framework outlined above, several key strategic questions—timing issues, product categories and number of licensees, distribution, payment structures, methods of keeping the property exciting over time—must all be resolved.

Timing

A licensor must select the best time to launch licensed products at retail. If the main objective is to support a long-term brand, a few key products may appear on the market first, followed by a slow expansion into related product categories. If, on the other hand, maximizing awareness and viewership for a relatively new show is the primary goal, a preferable strategy may be to simultaneously place a large number of different products in the marketplace, far enough after the show's launch so that consumer awareness of the show exists, yet fairly early in its life—before interest begins to fade. Or, if a new television show is based on an existing property with high awareness (e.g., a hit film), then merchandise may be placed at retail prior to the show's initial air date, to generate interest and possibly increase ratings for the premiere.

As mentioned earlier, several television licensing programs have failed because products reached stores *too* early. This is particularly true of weekly series, but also affects strips (shows aired Monday through Friday). If viewers are not familiar with a show, they are not going to purchase products. And, if merchandise does not sell right away, retailers will replace it with something else. Even if a show eventually becomes popular, it will be difficult to convince retailers to restock the merchandise; in their experience it was a failure, and they will be reluctant to get burned again.

Tiny Toon Adventures and *Thomas the Tank Engine* were two shows for which merchandise was in stores too early. Both of these programs managed to recover from their initial failure and eventually became successful. But in general, television licensors who launch their efforts too early will have a tough time creating a strong program, even when the time is right.

In addition to timing the launch of a licensing effort, licensors should also consider the program's rollout, or the speed and magnitude of its expansion. If virtually every possible product is available from day one, there will not be much room to expand into new categories later. This may be preferable for a property with a short window of opportunity, but could hurt the longevity of a potentially long-term brand.

Lead times between the initiation of the licensing effort and the appearance of products at retail are also critical. It takes time to select licensees and negotiate contracts with them; negotiations alone can take six to eight weeks. The product approval process, product development, manufacturing, and shipping all take time. The total span from contract signing to store shelves can be as long as a year and a half. Some products require longer periods to bring them to market than others; toys, video games, and footwear, for example, have lengthy lead times, while apparel tends to reach the marketplace more quickly. Thus, some product categories must be signed early because they require more time to arrive on retail shelves.

Selection of product categories

Toys, video games, apparel, accessories, gifts, paper goods, and publishing are some of the key categories where television-based licensing plays a role. Numerous other categories may be appropriate as well, however. Licensors are limited only by their imaginations and those of their licensees, as well as by the characteristics of their properties, when exploring product categories to enter.

The key criterion in determining what products are authorized should be the fit between the product and the property: they should have similar target audiences, demonstrate compatibility between property and product, and the licensor and licensee should possess similar objectives. The licensed merchandise has to make sense, not just to the partners, but to consumers as well. They must have a reason to buy the licensed product over a similar, generic version.

For children's properties, the sex of the target audience is one of the most important criteria for selecting product categories. Most television shows are targeted to children of both sexes, with a skew either to boys or girls. But in the case of merchandising, most successful programs target either one sex or the other (with the exception of pre-school programs). For instance, lots of girls watched the *Teenage Mutant Ninja Turtles*, but merchandise was targeted very strongly to boys. Licensing programs that try to reach both sexes equally tend to not work. (The Power Rangers seem to be an exception; girls buy Halloween costumes, toys and other products, particularly those based on Kimberly, the pink Ranger.)

The importance of "fit" can be illustrated by some examples. An educational science show for pre-teens would lend itself to science toys and games of all sorts, but may not necessarily be appropriate for paper partyware. A program that appeals to adults will lend itself to certain apparel items and gifts, but probably not footwear, even though that is a key category for animated children's properties. A property for teen males will include video games, but action figures may be detrimental to the property as a whole, since they bring down the target age too far. Not only will teenagers avoid the toys, but they may stay away from the electronic games as well, since the toys indicate to them that the property is meant for little boys, and therefore not "cool."

Some categories are important to a licensing program for reasons other than just because they make sense. For example, a major children's animation property depends heavily on toys—which can account for well over 50% of total retail sales—not just because they are appropriate for the target age group and generate significant sales, but because toy manufacturers spend a great deal of money on advertising (Figure 4.1). This advertising also indirectly promotes other licensed products based on the same property, and is an incentive for other manufacturers to join the program; they benefit from the awareness of the property, without having to advertise it themselves.

Similarly, video games can be a key category, especially for teens. Not only do they generate huge sales levels, but they are a form of entertainment in their own right. Therefore, players of the game feel more of a connection with the property, which may encourage them to purchase other categories of merchandise, and also to watch the television show more often. The same is true of other categories, such as publishing and home video. Apparel also is an important category for many programs, especially those targeted toward adults, since it serves as a walking billboard, providing promotional exposure for the property.

Number of licensees

Some properties have over 100 licensees, others have thirty or forty, while still others have just a few. The number of licensees does not correlate at all with total retail sales levels or with the number of

FIGURE 4.1 The Mighty Morphin Power Rangers stand guard over a wide range of licensed merchandise. The advertising and publicity surrounding toy licensee Bandai helps drive sales of other products from Halloween costumes to balloons.

™ and © Saban Entertainment, Inc. Used with permission.

products available at retail. Some 30-licensee properties surpass 100-plus-licensee programs both in the number of products available and in sales. The decision regarding how many licensees to sign is, rather, a strategic one. A single licensee can be authorized to make one or a few products or to manufacture a wide range of different products across many categories, as long as it has the production and distribution capability to do so.

If a primary objective is to maximize upfront revenues to help finance a show's production, authorizing many licensees—each making a relatively narrow product line—will probably lead to the largest amount of advance money. If the goal, on the other hand, is to create a controlled, long-term licensing program, signing a few trusted licensees, each with broad product capability and for whom the licensed line is an important part of their business, may be the best way to meet the objectives.

Distribution

There are many types of distribution channels. They include department stores, specialty stores—such as independent gift, book, or toy shops—mass merchants, mail order catalogs, and teleshopping.

The distribution tiers in which the licensed products are sold depend on the property's image. An upscale program, such as those based on HBO or CNN, would be limited primarily to department stores and specialty outlets (known as the "upstairs" market), whereas products based on an animated children's property such as the Ninja Turtles, for which maximizing exposure and revenues is important, would be found in mass merchants such as Target, Kmart, and Wal-Mart (the "downstairs" market).

In fact, an upscale brand may be hurt if products based on it find their way to mass merchants. If customers who watch a particular network or show because it appeals to them and fits their upscale lifestyle see products based on the brand at Wal-Mart or Kmart, they may begin to perceive the network as meant for a broad audience, and not for them specifically. In this case, while more products may be sold at the mass level, the licensing program has backfired because it has alienated the network's or show's core viewers.

The shopping habits of the target customer are also a factor, of course; if a television series' audience is mainly upscale, as would be true for many adult-targeted programs on PBS, for example, products in specialty and department stores would tend to move better than those on the shelves of mass retailers.

As licensors seek to maximize sales and exposure, they often try to expand into untapped distribution channels. Adding new distribution tiers has pros and cons, however. On the one hand, increased distribution can increase awareness for the property, driving sales across all channels. The Warner Bros. Studio Stores, for example, have been credited with driving Looney Tunes merchandise in all types of retail environments, not just in the Studio Stores themselves. On the other hand, existing retailers and manufacturers can feel threatened by this expansion. They may feel that their sales will be cannibalized, since their customers have the option of buying similar merchandise elsewhere. This perception could harm the licensor's relationship with its licensees and retailers.

There are ways to alleviate this problem, however. One method is to authorize different merchandise for each type of distribution channel. A customer would have to go to a department store to buy one style of shirt, for example, and to a mass retailer for another style, although both are based on the same property. Some licensors, such as Disney, have launched sub-brands (Mickey & Co. and Mickey Unlimited, for example), each targeted to a different distribution tier and different demographics.

Determining the terms of payment

A royalty is the basic element of payment for a license. The royalty—usually between 5% and 12% for entertainment properties—is typically payable on the net sales, or wholesale, price of the product. A minimum guaranteed royalty, or a "guarantee," is usually required. The guarantee protects the licensor from licensees who tie up a category but then do not adequately market the licensed merchandise. Of course, a guarantee, while greatly reducing the licensor's risk, adds more risk for the licensee, who is responsible for payment even if the license as a whole fails.

The minimum guarantee is a guarantee against royalties. That is, if royalties from actual sales do not reach the guarantee level by the end of the contract period, the licensee owes the licensor the remainder of the guarantee. If the guarantee is exceeded by actual royalties, no further money is owed. The guarantee level is generally set at a percentage—such as 50% to 75%—of forecasted royalties over the contract period. Part of the guarantee—varying widely but often in the 25% to 30% range—is usually paid as an advance, with the remainder payable at the end of the contract period, if still outstanding.

Royalties, advances, and guarantees all vary widely, depending on the situation. Guarantees, for example, can range from a few hundred dollars to millions. Why? First, the licensor's objectives play a role. If the licensor is hoping to partially fund a production with merchandising revenues, it may require high advances, as noted earlier. If the company is trying to attract licensees to an unproven property, guarantees might be low to minimize the licensee's risk and provide an incentive for it to sign on.

Supply and demand also play a role; a hit property, or a new property from a licensor with a track record of hits, can command high royalties, guarantees, and advances, while newer properties often cannot. Compensation also varies among licensees of the same property. Market considerations in licensees' respective industries, such as industry-average margins, affect the royalty rate, for example. Food marketers, which operate under low margins, pay a relatively low average royalty in the 2%–3% range, while fine-art poster makers, which tend to have much higher margins, pay a higher royalty percentage.

Similarly, a licensee with high product development costs or significant retooling requirements will probably negotiate a lower advance to compensate for this investment. And expected sales and price points affect guarantees as well, with producers of low-priced novelties paying lower guarantees than apparel manufacturers.

Promotional support

Licensees and retailers often make their decision to support a license based largely on the promotional plans behind it. Individual licensees may support the line with their own promotions, e.g., an event, a cross-merchandising deal with another licensee, or a contest. But the property itself is increasingly promoted by the licensor, as well, and this support is virtually a prerequisite before retailers will get behind a property.

Promotions can include a wide range of components, depending on the type of property, the goals of the licensor, and the funds and human resources available. The more innovative and unique the promotion, the better it will cut through the clutter in advertising and at the point of sale. Strong promotional elements help drive sales of licensed merchandise and also help build awareness for the property (Figure 4.2).

Licensors often provide retailers with signage and other point-of-purchase materials, help them create in-store concept shops that gather property-based merchandise from a variety of licensees, and help organize events—such as contests or personal appearances—that drive new customers into the stores.

FIGURE 4.2 Promotional support for Barney the Dinosaur, PBS star, includes an attraction at Universal Studios Florida, live appearances at venues such as Radio City Music Hall in New York, and an upcoming film.

© 1993 The Lyons Group. Photo Credit: Mark Perlstein.

Promotions with packaged goods companies can also add awareness to a property. These types of tie-ins can include coupons for discounted or free merchandise, sweepstakes or other contests, or cross-merchandising between the packaged goods product and licensees' merchandise. Packaged goods promotions introduce the marketing message into a new environment—grocery stores—and generate thousands of additional impressions.

Live events and other entertainment vehicles, such as mall and other live tours, personal appearances, films, and ice shows (e.g., the Looney Tunes star in a national touring ice show, licensed to Giant On Ice) are an additional method of keeping the television-based property fresh by allowing consumers to experience it in a new way. They can also provide opportunities to sell licensed merchandise on-site.

Most of the promotional tools outlined here are particularly prevalent at a property launch, such as the premiere of a new television show. They are also, however, increasingly utilized on other occasions as well. For example, anniversaries of the property (the 25th year since it was created, the 200th episode, the 100th anniversary of the birth of its creator) provide opportunities to promote the property, and can help drive licensed merchandise sales. The same holds true of new media vehicles (video games, films, home video releases, animated versions of live-action shows) and the introduction of new product lines.

All of these promotional elements are most successful if supported by advertising and publicity. Both licensees and licensors may advertise to the trade and consumer press, for example, increasing awareness of the licensed merchandise and the property itself. Trade magazine ads placed by licensors usually contain a licensee list and a summary of promotional plans.

Implementing a Licensing Program
Pitching a property to licensees

In order to convince a licensee to sign on to a property, licensors need to prove the value of the property. Manufacturers want complete information about the members of the property's target audience, such as their age, sex, and income, where they shop, what types of products they buy, and why they like the television show on which the licensing effort is based. How many fans there are and how this viewership has grown is also of interest. If the property is an existing one, sales information on other product lines and sales and attendance figures for related media vehicles is helpful to manufacturers; the more specific and measurable the information—sales figures on products, books, and videos; ratings history; box-office figures—the better a licensor will be able to sell the property's value.

A style book is also an important sales tool for licensors, as well as a guideline for the companies who ultimately become licensees. A style book illustrates the various trademarks and other property depictions available for use on products. It includes detailed specifications, including colors and dimensions, tips on how to draw logos and characters, and visuals of photographs and artwork available. It also often includes mock-ups or sketches of how the property can be incorporated into various products, such as notebooks, party goods, footwear, scarves, action figures, or plush (stuffed animals or figures). The style book also contains information on appropriate legal marking (e.g., trademark symbols and copyright notices and when they are to be used), as well as required hangtags (tags that hang from a garment or other product) and other labeling.

Even before the style book, some art reference materials must be provided to licensees *early*, so that the product development process can begin.

In addition to marketing and design information, a list of character attributes helps sell the property, particularly one that will extend into product categories such as original home videos, audio recordings, publishing, video games, and other products with literary or creative content. Character likes and dislikes, habits, and significant personality traits are all relevant to marketers in these categories.

Finally, the licensor should outline its plans for promotional and entertainment support. What future entertainment vehicles, such as films, home video, sequels, and specials are planned and when are they scheduled? Anticipated video-game releases and publishing schedules for magazines, books, and comic books will also assist potential licensees in getting a complete picture of the property. Definite and potential promotions should also be clearly outlined to licensees. Plans for packaged goods, retail, or fast-food promotions are attractive to licensees, as are extensive advertising schedules by licensors, live events, anniversary celebrations, and so on.

Selecting licensees

Once appropriate product categories have been identified, the process of selecting specific licensees begins. The quality of licensees' products, based on the sample merchandise they provide, is one important criterion in the decision about which manufacturer to select. Their typical price range should fit into the licensor's plans, and the product itself must have value: Are the toys fun to play with? Is the apparel fashionable? A good licensee should demonstrate the ability to keep the product line fresh from season to season, as well.

Distribution is another important factor in selecting a licensee. Manufacturers should have an existing retail customer base, consistent with the distribution tier targeted by the licensor, and should have good relationships with those retailers. Appropriate licensees should have a reputation for providing adequate support, shipping on time, and offering consistently high-quality merchandise.

The licensee's ability to translate the graphic elements of the property into a creative, saleable product line, without violating the constraints on how the trademarks can be used, is also a prerequisite. Its proposed licensed products should make sense with the property, appeal to the licensor's target customers, stand out from other products, and uphold the property's image. The licensee's manufacturing capacity, including physical plant and personnel, should be adequate to achieve expected sales in the territories and for the product lines authorized.

And, of course, licensees' financial stability is another important factor in the decision process. Their credit ratings, financial histories, payment histories to other property owners, and credit references should all meet licensors' standards. Finally, all other things being equal, a final tie-breaking criterion would be the amount each potential licensee is willing to pay in the form of royalties, advances, and guarantees. Monetary factors are rarely the only or the most important criterion, unless the *sole* objective of the licensing effort is to maximize upfront cash.

A number of methods of finding appropriate licensees exists. Several directories list licensees and what products they produce, as well as representative licenses held. Licensing trade publications, as well as trade journals in all of the industries where licensing is a significant marketing tool, all give licensors a sense of who the major licensees are and what they are up to. Attending trade shows in various product categories is also a good way to keep abreast of licensing developments. Finally, sending publicity releases to and advertising in trade publications, as well as exhibiting at the annual licensing trade show in New York, will allow licensors' properties to become known to potential licensees. (The Appendixes provide further information on these resources.)

To evaluate potential licensees, most licensors use a licensee evaluation or application form. On the form, licensees provide information on their company size, personnel and manufacturing capabilities; past sales records for licensed and non-licensed products; sales forecasts and marketing plans for the licensed line under consideration; current retail distribution and major retail customers; top competitors; financial information; and trade and credit references. Licensors also require samples of past merchandise and sometimes prototypes of proposed licensed products, as well as samples of planned ancillary marketing materials. Supplementary information such as merchandise catalogs, annual reports, and brochures also helps in the decision-making process.

Product approvals

A faulty product can cause irreparable damage to a property's image, especially if the defect harms a child. Thus, quality control is an extremely important facet of a licensing program. The best protection against poor quality is the careful selection of appropriate licensees; a second tool is the product approval process. Licensees submit samples at various stages of manufacturing, each of which the licensor then approves or disapproves. The licensee then has the opportunity to correct the problem if it is able to. Some licensors take the approval process more seriously than others, and while it can take a long time and be somewhat annoying to the licensee, a rigorous approval policy actually protects both parties by ensuring that the best—and most marketable—products end up in stores. It also helps maintain a consistent brand image from item to item, thus strengthening the property and merchandise associated with it.

Selling to retailers

Selling licensed products to retailers—ensuring that the merchandise appears on store shelves on schedule—is primarily the responsibility of manufacturers. After all, the licensor selected its licensees in part because of their ability to sell to the retailers most appropriate for the property.

As noted earlier, however, support from licensors is critical to this effort. Many licensors meet directly with marketing and buying personnel at key retailers about nine to twelve months prior to the launch of a property (or prior to a scheduled promotion) to help explain the concept of the license, to promote a cohesive brand image across all products, and to encourage the retailer to merchandise the products together in an in-store boutique. Some licensors bring key manufacturers with them on these sales calls.

Licensors can assist licensees in selling to retailers by organizing retail promotions in regional markets, as well as nationally. Offering exclusive products to a retailer or arranging a broad store-wide promotion will increase overall awareness of the property, encourage sales within those stores, and provide an incentive to retailers to get behind the property. Of course, all promotional activities supporting the property, even those not specifically related to a given store or chain of stores, will increase the chances that a retailer will buy licensed merchandise.

Combating counterfeiting

Finding and stopping counterfeiters—manufacturers who sell unauthorized merchandise incorporating a licensed property—is a big problem, especially for popular properties. Combating infringement requires constant vigilance on the part of the licensor, as well as a significant commitment of funds and personnel. Licensees are paying licensors for the right to use a trademark with value; counterfeiting decreases the mark's worth. A property's image could be hurt when poor-quality goods invade the market, and counterfeit goods also cut into sales of legitimate merchandise. Therefore, a strong anti-infringement program by licensors makes their marks more attractive to licensees.

Requiring licensees to use consistent packaging and labeling that identifies the merchandise as an official licensed product makes unauthorized merchandise easier to spot in the field, and is thus an effective tool in an anti-counterfeiting program. Occasionally, licensees are required to use holographic hangtags; while counterfeiters are able to duplicate them, it is prohibitively expensive to do so. (These devices are also expensive for licensees, however.)

Publicity and advertising targeted to licensees, retailers, and even consumers encourages them to report any incidences of infringement that they notice, and also alerts counterfeiters that licensors will not let them get away with illegal activities. Trade and consumer ads, publicity releases detailing successful anti-counterfeiting activities, and setting up 800 numbers to enable retailers, licensees, and customers to easily report infringement can all be effective.

If counterfeiting activity is discovered—through information from one of the sources mentioned above, by private investigators, or by U.S. Customs as unauthorized merchandise crosses the border—licensors can take several actions. First, they can try to transform the pirate into a licensee. Often, companies are not aware that they have to pay a royalty or acquire permission to use an image. If this is the case, a deal can often be forged. If not, cease-and-desist letters, in which an attorney threatens legal action if the counterfeiter does not stop its illegal activity immediately, are usually the first step. Although these letters alone often do the trick, licensors should be prepared to act on their threats if necessary.

If court action is required, possible outcomes include seizures of merchandise and machinery, injunctions or restraining orders, fines, imprisonment, and monetary damages and penalties. The main goal of an anti-infringement effort is to take the steps, after weighing the costs and benefits of all options, that minimize the chance of future counterfeiting. Stopping illegal activity is a higher priority than receiving compensation, as a rule.

Using a licensing agent

Many property owners, especially when first launching a licensing effort, retain a licensing agent to handle merchandising activities for them. Licensing agents can provide several benefits, particularly to new licensors.

First, they have expertise. They maintain contacts throughout the industry, and their experience enables them to help a licensor set up a strategy, select licensees, and police its trademarks.

Licensing agents know how to negotiate a licensing contract, and they can help administer the licensing program, assisting the licensor in collecting royalties, moving the product approval process along, and staying in contact with licensees. Licensing agents are normally paid by commission (usually between 25% and 40%) of all licensing receipts.

Some property owners maintain their relationship with a single agent for a long period of time; others use a different agent for each of their properties. Still others use an agent to help them launch a licensing program, and take it in-house when that action becomes cost effective and logical. Some licensors, of course, do not use agents at all.

Lists of licensing agents can be found in the directories listed in the Appendixes. When selecting an agent, licensors should consider whether the agent has experience with television or entertainment properties. How did the agent handle various properties in the past? Its strategies should parallel the licensor's plans for its property. Talking to other current clients can also be revealing.

The number of properties the agent represents and the size of its company can be relevant factors in the decision-making process. Licensing agents range from individuals representing one or a few properties to fairly large organizations handling a large number of properties. Larger agencies may have more experience, more resources, and possibly more contacts, but a smaller agent may dedicate a significant amount of its time and effort to a property.

The Licensing Contract

A licensing agreement is simply a contract between the licensee and licensor that outlines the various rights and responsibilities of each partner. While the specifics of virtually every point are normally negotiable, based on the situation and advice of each partner's counsel, several standard items should be included in the agreement.

First, the contract should outline in detail what property or aspects of a property are involved. For example, can the licensee use character likenesses or only a television show's logo? It should also state explicitly what products are to be manufactured under the agreement, at what price points and distribution tier, and in what geographic territory. And, is the agreement exclusive or non-exclusive? All of these elements are known collectively as the "grant of rights."

The contract should specify the term, or length of the contract—usually two to three years but varying depending on the circumstances—as well as what happens at the end of the contract period. Some contracts grant an option to renew if certain performance levels are met; others do not. Also, what constitutes grounds for terminating the contract early? Failure to meet any of the terms of the agreement, such as paying royalties, introducing and marketing products on time, and staying within the allotted grant of rights, are likely to be grounds for termination. Finally, it is important to specify what happens after termination. A sell-off period is usually granted, for example, allowing a licensee to divest itself of excess inventory on a non-exclusive basis for a certain period of time, such as thirty days.

Naturally, compensation is outlined in the contract, including royalty rates, minimum guarantee amounts, and advances. Allowable deductions—billable items that do not require royalty payments, such as freight or reserves for returns—should be specified, if any. In addition, all terms that may be confusing should be defined. Auditing procedures should also be included to ensure the licensor's ability to monitor royalty payments.

The agreement should lay out in detail the product approval procedure, including how long the licensor has to approve the product at various steps in the manufacturing process—approvals are usually required at the concept, pre-production, and production stages—and how long the licensee has to fix the problems, if any.

Both partners must warrant in the agreement that they are capable of fulfilling the responsibilities outlined in the contract. The licensor must also indemnify, or protect, the licensee from any infringement claims brought by third parties. Meanwhile, the licensee must indemnify the licensor from product liability or personal injury suits brought against the licensed product. An insurance provision, in which the licensee names the licensor as the co-insured on specified insurance policies, backs up the indemnification. The contract also states who has the right and responsibility to bring suit against counterfeiters, who bears the costs of such actions, and who reaps the rewards, if any.

While this list summarizes many of the most important provisions, it is by no means comprehensive. Other items are often added, depending on the specific situation and the advice of both parties' legal counsel.

How to Evaluate a Property's Licensing Potential

It is difficult to evaluate the economic potential of a licensing program, in part because there are so many intangibles involved. Some properties that were expected to be a very tough sell became surprise hits—the Power Rangers and the Ninja Turtles, for example—while others that were thought by those in the business to have great potential died on retail shelves.

The best way to estimate how a property might do is to compare it to similar historical examples. Retail or wholesale sales figures for properties are sometimes available in back issues of consumer and trade publications—an online computer search is helpful in seeking such figures—or are generally known throughout the licensing community and can be ascertained through a licensing agent or another member of the licensing community.

The best comparisons are made by choosing a similar property; that is, an entertainment property with the same media and entertainment vehicles, promotional support, and target audience as are planned for the television-based effort to which it is being compared. It is important to be realistic, as well. Most properties are not "the next Mickey Mouse" or "the next Barney."

Licensors should also remember that their revenues are based on royalties, not retail sales. Total retail sales of $500 million over two years, for example, translates into $250 million wholesale (at a 50% average retail markup), with royalty income of approximately $17.5 million (at 7%). Still a nice income, but there is a big difference between $17 million and a half billion.

Chapter 5

Case Studies

The case studies in this chapter illustrate many of the concepts and trends outlined throughout the book. Each of the five real-life examples is widely considered successful; it should be noted that not every television-based licensing effort will generate the sales levels associated with these shows. The examples do, however, demonstrate how individual strategies vary, depending on the characteristics of the property and the objectives of the licensor. In addition, they highlight some similarities between otherwise diverse licensing programs.

Beverly Hills 90210

The *Beverly Hills 90210* licensing effort is an example of one targeted toward a niche market—teens—that many marketers find difficult to reach. It illustrates some of the challenges associated with launching a new licensing program, and how they can be overcome if grassroots demand for the show—and for licensed merchandise based on it—is strong. In addition, its significant international component is indicative of the potential for overseas markets to generate sales of licensed merchandise based on United States–originated television programming.

Selling a new property to licensees

Beverly Hills 90210 went on the air in October 1990. In February 1991, Hamilton Projects, licensing agent for the show's producer,

Spelling Entertainment, began to seek out licensees for the property. (Spelling purchased Hamilton later that year.)

The series' share of viewership at the time was about 8%, and it had not received much notice from the media except for reviews—mostly pans. Still, teen magazines were being inundated with fan mail about the show, demonstrating that there was a market for licensed merchandise targeted toward the hard-to-reach teen segment.

From February through June of 1991, however, there was very little interest in *90210* on the part of licensees and retailers. Spelling and Hamilton Projects offered licenses at a low cost in order to get the ball rolling, but except for a couple of licensees who made an early commitment (including Spencer Gifts, a retail chain, and O.S.P., a poster and button manufacturer), interest was still low. First, the program targeted teenagers, who are a notoriously fickle audience; with occasional exceptions, such as the New Kids On The Block, few licensed properties aimed at teens demonstrate success. Second, live-action shows are generally more difficult to license than animation; images are graphically harder to incorporate into merchandise, and acquiring rights to actors' likenesses can be a challenge.

Despite the lack of interest, though, Hamilton continued to lay the groundwork for the property by making presentations and explaining the property's attributes. Thus, when ratings began to rise, and demand for products started to grow, potential licensees and retailers already knew about and understood the property. Hamilton and Spelling were therefore poised to act quickly when demand for the property became evident.

That began to happen in summer 1991. The Fox network aired new episodes of the show during a traditional rerun season, which caused ratings to rise (up to a 20 share by fall) and garnered significant press coverage. Fox's strategy of starting its season in July (rather than in September with the rest of the networks) gave Fox shows, including *90210*, the opportunity to attract an audience. Licensees began to sign on, and retailers wanted merchandise in stores in time for Christmas. Rights clearances had been obtained for a library of 100 photographs, which enabled licensees to create merchandise with a variety of designs; footwear, apparel, and other products began appearing on store shelves in the fall of 1991 (Figure 5.1). Macy's gathered the merchandise into in-store

FIGURE 5.1   Clearances obtained from the actors in *Beverly Hills 90210*
enabled licensees to choose from a library of 100 photographs for graphics to
incorporate into products.
© Spelling Entertainment.

boutiques for Christmas of that year, and J.C. Penney ran a
90210 promotion, also featuring concept shops, for Valentine's
Day 1992.

The fact that the show was on the air for nearly a year before
products hit the market was not planned, but turned out to
be a benefit. It lessened the risk for licensees, and it allowed
the series time to come into its own. Ultimately, a total of about
seventy or eighty domestic licensees were involved with the
program.

Licensing strategy

By early 1992, the target demographics of the property began to expand downward. First targeted toward ages 14 and up, the program first expanded as low as age 12 and soon thereafter down to ages 8 to 12. Apparel, accessories, and footwear anchored the program in the United States, but there were other important categories as well. For example, in the spring of 1992, fashion dolls by Mattel were introduced to meet the demand of the younger consumers. Calendars, fragrances, books, and magazines were also important.

Some categories were intentionally avoided, such as 900 numbers (popular promotional tools for licensed properties at that time, although they have since waned). Children's cosmetics were also waived in favor of a real fragrance line, which, as of this writing, is still sold at Wal-Mart.

From the beginning, the licensing program was expected to have a two-year life cycle, given the nature of the target market. As of Christmas 1992 (eighteen months after the first merchandise was introduced), products were still selling, having generated a total of $250 million at retail in licensed merchandise in the United States thus far. That far into the life cycle, however, sales were expected to start falling off. Extending the licensing program would have led to the risk of bloated inventories by licensees if demand dropped precipitously.

In addition, the company was preparing its off-network syndication efforts for *90210*, and it was decided that the licensing program would harm rather than enhance what would already be a difficult task. The continued presence of licensed merchandise in stores may have supported the perception that the show was a teen fad. In order to make it attractive to stations, it had to be positioned as having broader demographic appeal.

Third, extending the licensing program—if it led to excess inventory in the United States—could have led to the dumping of products overseas, particularly in Europe. That situation would have hurt the licensing program abroad, which was still in its early stages. Thus, based on the overall objectives of the company, it was decided that extending the licensing program would have been more harmful than helpful. Although contracts for a few products were extended, such as the branded fragrances and eyewear (both of which are still selling in the fall of 1994) and posters, most licenses were allowed to expire.

Promotional activity

Beverly Hills 90210 was described to potential tie-in partners as a good way to reach the elusive teen market. The willingness of the show's stars to participate in promotions was also a benefit. In order to prevent market oversaturation, however, the number of tie-ins was limited to two per quarter starting in the fall of 1991, and just one of those was supported by television advertising. In total, eleven promotional partners were involved with the property, including Procter & Gamble's Noxzema brand, Sassaby cosmetic carrying cases, General Mills' Honey Nut Cheerios, Coca-Cola Foods' Hi-C brand, Alberto-Culver's Bold-Hold hair-styling product, Mentholatum's Softlips brand, Conair's California Shine hair care line, Coca-Cola (in-store at United Artists theaters), and SmithKline Beecham's Oxy acne treatment product.

In most of the promotions, actors and actresses from the show appeared in ads and in live appearances, trips to the set were awarded, and licensed merchandise was offered as a premium. In addition, point-of-sale materials, as well as advertising, enhanced awareness of the show among potential viewers.

International expansion

In total, retail sales of *90210* licensed merchandise worldwide surpassed $500 million, with slightly more than half attributable to overseas markets. The show rolled out internationally approximately twelve to fourteen months after its U.S. debut, although the timing varied market by market. The United Kingdom was an exception; the show was launched there simultaneously with the U.S. launch.

While there was some resistance on the part of licensing sub-agents, licensees, and retailers toward the property overseas, for the same reasons that it was initially a tough sell in the United States, the fact that it had a U.S. track record meant that merchandise was able to reach international retail much closer to the show's launch than it had in the United States. In fact, Hamilton Projects and its network of international agents particularly wanted to ensure that a large publisher in each market had books available at retail in conjunction with the show's launch.

In terms of product categories, there were some differences between the U.S. and overseas markets. Publishing was very strong in Europe (which is typical for most entertainment-related licensing programs). For example, two million hardcover books sold in Germany at a price of $16, Italy accounted for one million book purchases, and three *90210* books were in the top ten at the same time in The Netherlands, according to Hamilton Projects. The dolls, in general, did more poorly overseas than they did in the United States. Apparel was strong internationally, particularly in Southeast Asia, where branded apparel with a very small *90210* logo was merchandised in Gap-like *90210* shops. The core age group of the show's fans also varied from market to market.

Overall, Mattel sold $50 million in dolls, or about 10% of worldwide retail sales of *90210* merchandise (which is a relatively low percentage for a licensing program geared to children). Thirteen books by HarperCollins sold more than eight million copies, and $50 million worth of cosmetics and fragrances sold worldwide.

Europe accounted for 65%–75% of non-U.S. revenues from sales of licensed *Beverly Hills 90210* merchandise. Australia/New Zealand was also a strong territory, with $20–$25 million in sales (for a market of seventeen million people). As of fall 1994, the two-year property life cycle was approaching its final stages in most territories, although a few products were still selling worldwide.

Thomas the Tank Engine

The Thomas the Tank Engine licensing program is representative of the relatively new-found strength of PBS as a source of licensed properties; this is the first PBS show since *Sesame Street* to have a wide-ranging licensing effort. The Thomas program also illustrates the learning curve that occurs when launching a new licensing effort. Furthermore, it emphasizes the importance of choosing the appropriate distribution tier within the context of the licensing strategy.

Thomas's launch in the United States

Thomas the Tank Engine & Friends was created as a television show in the United Kingdom in 1984 by producer Britt Allcroft. Based on a series of stories by the Reverend Wilbert Awdry written from 1948 to 1972, the television version runs in Britain as an eleven-minute segment comprising two Thomas episodes. It generated a great deal of licensing activity, starting with puzzles and building to a range of children's products in England, Australia, and New Zealand.

The series caught the notice of WNET, New York's public television station, which at the time was interested in strengthening its children's programming lineup. As a result, Britt Allcroft and her new production partner Rick Siggelkow developed a half-hour program for American children called *Shining Time Station*. Each show incorporated five-and-a-half-minute episodes of the British films starring Thomas, a steam engine, and his friends. The series was distributed to public television stations by the Public Broadcasting System starting in January 1989.

At the same time, a licensing program was also launched in the United States. The merchandise focused exclusively on the Thomas vignettes, rather than on the other *Shining Time Station* characters. (A completely separate *Shining Time Station* program was launched later.)

The learning curve

Initially, attracting the interest of licensees and retailers was a challenge for a number of reasons. First, the program was distributed on PBS stations, competing with network and syndicated fare that generally attracts larger audiences. Aside from *Sesame Street*, PBS was an unproven distribution channel for broad-based licensing programs, and furthermore, Thomas was a pre-school (age 3–7, to be exact) property rather than one targeted toward the major buyers of licensed merchandise, children aged 5–11. Finally, licensees thought that children in the United States would not be interested in steam trains, in spite of the success of the merchandising program in the United Kingdom (where ten million licensed Thomas books sold in the first year alone).

The licensees that were signed concentrated on the mass market, and merchandise became widely available. But despite good reviews, favorable press coverage, and a good-sized PBS audience, products did not move. According to the *Wall Street Journal*, sales of licensed merchandise totaled less than $2 million in 1989.

Specializing in the upstairs market

As a result of slow early sales, Britt Allcroft Inc. (whose U.S. arm was known at the time as Quality Family Entertainment) rethought its strategy. The company was receiving letters from viewers saying that they were seeking Thomas products at their local toy stores but could not find any merchandise. Based on the fact that mass market licensees tend to underserve the low-volume specialty market, as well as the fact that the PBS audience is primarily composed of an upscale demographic group, the company decided to refocus its efforts on the specialty market, particularly independent toy stores, starting in 1990 (Figure 5.2).

Licensees were still somewhat reluctant to sign on, based on the property's early track record, as well as the reasons noted above.

FIGURE 5.2 Sales of licensed merchandise based on Thomas the Tank Engine began to take off once the distribution strategy for the property was refocused, with products targeted exclusively to the upstairs market.
Britt Allcroft (Thomas) Limited 1986.

(Britt Allcroft management theorizes that products may have been in the market too early, as well as being in the wrong distribution tier.) During the fourth quarter of 1991, however, grassroots demand from parents of pre-schoolers blossomed, and product shortages ensued, piquing licensees' interest. Even after the property became successful enough to again attract the notice of mass market licensees, however, the company decided to remain with manufacturers who specialize in the upstairs market (specialty and department stores), and continues to stick with that plan for the Thomas program.

With upstairs distribution in place and consumer demand high, the *Wall Street Journal* reported that sales of licensed merchandise reached the $200 million mark in 1992, according to industry estimates, and *Forbes* estimated that licensed merchandise based on the property had generated cumulative retail sales of $750 million as of the end of 1993. (The privately held Britt Allcroft does not release sales figures.)

Strategic considerations

Britt Allcroft plans its licensing effort on a three-year cycle (paralleling the typical length of licensing contracts), and tries to maintain that schedule in terms of when promotions and expansion to new categories should occur. The company intended to manage Thomas as a long-term property from the beginning, which, says management, means saying no to some interested licensees if the time is not right.

Key product categories for Thomas are those that help enhance a child's relationship with the property. For example, home video and publishing are important, because they further the storylines and allow children to interact with the characters when they are not watching the television program. And toys, particularly toy trains, are important because they allow children to incorporate the property into their play.

Expansion into new categories is based to a large extent on requests from consumers who write in to the company asking if certain products are available and where they can find them. Not every request is answered with a new line of merchandise, of course, but new products are rarely considered if there has not been a demonstrated interest from consumers. In addition to the core categories, Thomas merchandise includes apparel, pajamas, flashlights, greeting cards, party goods, and more, manufactured by about seventy-five licensees.

Promotions have also been an important part of the Thomas licensing strategy. In 1991, an appearance at the New York City Bloomingdale's flagship store attracted 14,000 people, and in 1992 a similar event attracted 25,000 people. A traveling mall show called *Shining Time Station—Live!* features music, dance, story-telling, and audience participation. Individual retailers also promote Thomas with concept shops, contests, giveaways, and special displays. (Licensed products based on the property are not television advertised.)

Britt Allcroft looks at itself as a producer, rather than a licensor, preferring to call the creation of products "off-screen production" rather than licensing. The income generated from merchandising is important, says the company, in that it provides the ability for it to remain independent and preserves its creative freedom: "We make money because we make magic, but we can only go on making magic if we make money." And, in terms of awareness, licensing creates a link between the consumer and the property, spreading the word about the show and strengthening viewership.

Nickelodeon

Nickelodeon was a pioneer among cable networks in terms of utilizing licensing as a technique to generate awareness for its brand, and was also among the first to offer its original programming to potential licensees. In addition to illustrating the differences between branded and show-specific licensing strategies, Nickelodeon's licensing effort is also a good example of the increasing level of intra-company synergy demonstrated by large entertainment companies.

Early cable licensing

Nickelodeon was one of the first cable networks to license out its own original programming and its brand name. It set up a licensing department in 1990—eleven years after the launch of the network—and began licensing *Double Dare*, a game show format, followed shortly by *Eureeka's Castle*, a show starring puppets. Nickelodeon branded licensing began in 1991 with the signing of

Mattel as the worldwide master toy licensee for activity toys, making Nickelodeon-oriented products such as Gak, Green Slime, and later Floam. Branded products from other licensees include sports-related toys, including a NERF/Nickelodeon co-branded line from Hasbro, computer accessories, gifts, footwear, watches and clocks, sunglasses and other eyewear, buttons, books, electronics, and home video and audio, the latter from licensee Sony Wonder.

In addition, Nickelodeon is launching branded licensing efforts based on some of its sub-brands, such as Nick Jr. for younger children and Nick at Nite. The latter program will focus primarily on department and specialty store distribution, and will comprise branded products targeted at the teens and adults that watch Nick at Nite's lineup of nostalgic sitcoms, including *Mary Tyler Moore*, *I Love Lucy*, *Bob Newhart*, *Bewitched*, *I Dream of Jeannie*, *Dick Van Dyke*, *Get Smart*, and others.

In addition to *Double Dare* and *Eureeka's Castle*, Nickelodeon has licensed several other original programs. *Ren & Stimpy*, Nickelodeon's largest show-specific effort, currently counts twenty-four domestic and twenty international companies as licensees, making everything from gifts to apparel to paper products. Other current shows with licensing programs of various magnitudes include *Clarissa Explains It All*, *Doug*, *Fifteen* (for publishing only), *Rocko's Modern Life*, *Rugrats*, and *Wienerville*.

A total of more than forty-five licensees are currently signed for all Nickelodeon properties (brands and shows).

Show-specific vs. branded strategies

Although the core values of the network govern both the program-specific and branded licensing efforts—which means that there are certain consistent elements between the two—strategies for each differ slightly. Merchandising programs for individual shows such as *Rocko* or *Ren & Stimpy* are shorter term because of the cyclical nature of demand for merchandise based on them. In addition, the products are associated primarily with the personalities and look of the characters themselves, rather than on any particular brand attributes. These types of licensing efforts require flexibility and the ability to act quickly to capitalize on demand when a character suddenly becomes popular.

Branded merchandise, on the other hand, reflects the essence of the network, and represents all the programming on Nickelodeon.

It is less straightforward to translate that essence to a shirt or a toy than it is to capture the look and feel of an individual character; thus, the network is careful not to introduce products until it feels they do reflect the attributes of the brand. This slow-and-steady approach contrasts with show-specific licensing, where launching products in time to meet maximum demand is crucial.

Nickelodeon maintains several guidelines for creating branded products. For example, in the case of toys and games, the merchandise must be as genderless as possible, there must be no wrong or right way to play with it, it must incorporate open-ended play, and it must, in general, support the message that "you're fine just the way you are." Mattel's 1994 product introduction, Floam, meets these criteria; it also floats, bounces, makes noise, is tactile, and encourages active play. (Floam began appearing on top-selling toy lists in fall of 1994, and its sister product Gak has sold more than ten million units thus far). (Figure 5.3)

The role of licensing

Nickelodeon's approach to licensing is quite conservative, particularly with regard to branded merchandise but also—in comparison with many licensors—with its program-specific efforts. Its Nickelodeon branded apparel line is a good example: it is planned for 1995 launch, four years after the introduction of the first Nickelodeon toys. Eighteen months were devoted to figuring out what the line should look like, what type of retail distribution it should have, and what types of clothing should be included in it. Although the company was approached by several interested apparel licensees over the years, it wanted to wait until its strategy was honed. Nickelodeon's president and other top management were involved in the line's development.

Nickelodeon is also conservative in its approach to what product categories it will license, even for its original programming. For example, some items that are standard on most children's character/entertainment licensee rosters will not be authorized by Nickelodeon, including rack toys (small impulse purchases that are displayed on racks at retail), shoe laces, and merchandise it considers faddish, such as milk caps (a currently popular collectible toy).

The network perceives licensing as both a method of brand enhancement and a revenue generator. It is important to Nickelodeon to create licensed merchandise that provides off-air enter-

FIGURE 5.3 Products based on the Nickelodeon brand include Gak Splat,
marketed by licensee Mattel.

Courtesy of Nickelodeon.

tainment and fashion to current viewers, as well as products that
reach beyond core cable constituencies, thereby marketing the
brand to non-viewers.

Partnerships

The merger in 1994 of Viacom, Nickelodeon's parent company, and
Hollywood studio Paramount has led to more opportunities for
partnerships between Nickelodeon's properties and the network's
sister companies. One significant development is the transforma-
tion of the children's areas of the Paramount Theme Parks into
Nickelodeon-themed attractions. In addition, sister company

Viacom New Media is working with Nickelodeon on interactive software, and Simon & Schuster, another Viacom company, has entered into a multidivisional partnership with Nickelodeon to develop original book series and books based on the Nickelodeon brand, as well as Nick at Nite's classic television shows. All of these partnerships add exposure to the brand and the network's characters, enhancing the number of impressions generated by programming alone. (According to the network, Nickelodeon currently reaches 2- to 15-year-olds in sixty million U.S. households, or 63% of all U.S. television homes, and has 92% brand awareness among kids 6–17.)

Other Nickelodeon efforts that enhance awareness and provide promotional opportunities for the network and associated merchandise include Nickelodeon Studios at Universal Studios Florida and *Nickelodeon* magazine, which currently has a circulation of 500,000. Two live tours also enhance the brand's marketing efforts.

The network also looks at its relationships with licensees as partnerships. In fact, very few licensees are just licensees; most also have other relationships with Nickelodeon, such as advertising on the network or in the magazine, acting as long-term promotional partners, or serving as partners in other business ventures. Nickelodeon stresses partnerships with licensees and with retailers, working with them on all aspects of the licensing program, from product development, marketing, and advertising to promotions and retail merchandising. Therefore, goals and values on the part of licensees that parallel those of Nickelodeon are a crucial aspect of the decision about which manufacturers to select as licensees in the first place.

Hanna-Barbera Classic Animation

Like the Nickelodeon case study above, the Hanna-Barbera licensing effort is indicative of the trend toward increasing cooperation and partnerships among the various arms of large entertainment companies. It is also an example of the potential of licensing to help rejuvenate classic properties from the 1950s, '60s, and '70s, introducing them to new audiences while maintaining their appeal for nostalgic adults.

History of the studio

The creation of the first made-for-television cartoons, a cat and dog duo named Ruff and Reddy who appeared in 1957, marked the launch of Hanna-Barbera. William Hanna and Joe Barbera were already known for the cartoon characters they created for films, notably Tom and Jerry. But Ruff and Reddy were the first in a stable of over a thousand original television cartoons that came out of the Hanna-Barbera studio. The company is still producing original programming, including *Swat Kats* and 2 *Stupid Dogs*.

Hanna-Barbera was particularly prolific in the late 1950s, the 1960s, and the early 1970s. Following Ruff and Reddy in the 1950s were Huckleberry Hound (1957) and Quick Draw McGraw (1959). The 1960s brought the Flintstones (1960), Yogi Bear (1960), Snagglepuss (1960), the Jetsons (1962), Magilla Gorilla and Peter Potamus (1963), the Banana Splits (1968), Scooby Doo (1969), and Dick Dastardly and Muttley (who debuted in *Wacky Races* in 1969). The 1970s were marked by Josie and the PussyCats, based on Archie Comics characters (1970).

Other characters in the Hanna-Barbera library, some of whom were born as cartoon shorts making appearances in longer-format programs, include Top Cat, Augie Doggie and Doggie Daddy, Snooper and Blabber, Atom Ant, Secret Squirrel, Hong Kong Phooey, Wally Gator, Pixie and Dixie and Mr. Jinks, Ricochet Rabbit, Touché Turtle, Space Ghost, Penelope Pitstop, Hokey Wolf, Shazzan, Breezly and Sneezly, the Impossibles, and Birdman and the Galaxy Trio.

Early licensing

Many of the major Hanna-Barbera characters attracted significant licensing activity in the 1960s and 1970s, including Ruff and Reddy, the Flintstones, the Jetsons, Huckleberry Hound, Quick Draw McGraw, Scooby Doo, Wacky Races, Magilla Gorilla, and Peter Potamus. A small sampling of the many licensees of that period includes Ideal (toys), Milton-Bradley (games), Aladdin (lunch boxes), Ben Cooper (Halloween costumes), Dell (comic books), and Western Publishing (storybooks).

Some products came on the market by virtue of the fact that the programs had sponsors who were consumer goods companies and manufactured merchandise based on the programs that they sponsored. Ideal Toy, for example, financed Magilla Gorilla and Peter Potamus, while Kellogg sponsored Huckleberry Hound. The 1960s were also notable for the launch of two Flintstones products that are still on the market today: Miles Flintstones vitamins and Post Pebbles cereals.

In those early days, licensing was viewed as a way to provide an ancillary revenue stream. The studio's focus was on production and on getting the shows on the air; licensed products were developed on a case-by-case basis as manufacturers approached the company, rather than through a concerted strategy. Quality control was not a big concern, either, and products from the 1960s—such as red versions of Dino the Dinosaur, the Flintstones' purple pet—would never pass the product approval process in today's world (Figures 5.4, 5.5, and 5.6).

In the 1980s, the studio retained a licensing agent to oversee its program. Most activity focused on the Flintstones and, in conjunction with a feature film release in 1987, the Jetsons. Neither franchise drove significant licensed merchandise sales during the decade, however, according to Hanna-Barbera.

Developing a branded approach

In December of 1991, Hanna-Barbera was purchased by Turner Broadcasting System (TBS) and incorporated into its multi-company entertainment organization. Turner Licensing & Merchandising, a division of Turner Home Entertainment, then took over licensing responsibilities for the studio. The current strategy being implemented by Turner Licensing & Merchandising, as Hanna-Barbera's licensing agent, is to look at each character or group of characters as a long-term brand, and to identify which elements of the vast library of characters have the best potential for merchandising and new entertainment vehicles.

The licensing efforts that are given priority are those associated with major new entertainment. The Flintstones, for example, were the primary focus in 1994 when the live-action film, produced by Amblin Entertainment and distributed by Universal Pictures, was released. While the licensing program generated significant merchandise sales—reportedly $1 billion at retail worldwide for both classic- and film-related merchandise, with the vast majority attributable to the classic animated characters—another significant ele-

FIGURES 5.4 AND 5.5   Fred Flintstone and Barney Rubble toys from Marx Toys, 1963. Marx is still a Flintstones licensee.

© 1994 Hanna-Barbera Productions, Inc.

FIGURE 5.6   In contrast to the products of the 1960s, a group of modern
Hanna-Barbera products marketed by licensee Fossil is indicative of the level of
quality control required today.

© 1994 Hanna-Barbera Productions, Inc.

ment of the film in terms of merchandising was to create awareness
for the property and to provide the opportunity to relaunch the
Flintstones as a long-term brand. The film will be followed up by a
35th anniversary celebration of the characters in 1995. (While
MCA/Universal Merchandising, Amblin, and Turner Licensing &
Merchandising jointly handled licensing for the live-action film,
MCA/Universal had exclusive promotional rights for the film and
Turner had exclusive rights to Hanna-Barbera's classic cartoon ver-
sion of the Flintstones.)

Along similar strategic lines, 1996 has been dubbed by the
studio "the year of Jonny Quest," with a feature film and various
promotional events in the works. Jonny Quest will thus be a major
focus for licensing, with plans in development as of this writing.
Meanwhile, the emphasis on Jonny Quest also offers opportunities
for other properties within the library. For example, a "Hero Battalion" brand of licensed merchandise is being developed to tie in

some of the lesser-known action-oriented characters with the action-adventure film. The "Hero Battalion" will have its own branded logo, and will incorporate classic Hanna-Barbera characters such as Atom Ant, Space Ghost, Birdman and the Galaxy Trio, and the Herculoids, most of which would not have significant merchandising potential on their own.

Aside from the properties that are emphasized due to their connection with entertainment vehicles, Turner's staff identifies potential areas for licensing activity based on other characters in the library. Most of the products are gift items or social expressions (such as T-shirts, mugs, and greeting cards), targeted to adults for whom the properties have nostalgic appeal, and are sold primarily through department and specialty stores. For example, Dick Dastardly and Muttley have garnered several apparel licensees and have entered into a joint agreement with NASCAR auto racing for merchandise including apparel, accessories, and trading cards. (Dastardly and Muttley, incidentally, are as of this writing among the most popular characters in Japan.)

Intra-company synergy

Besides creating a branded outlook on licensing, the acquisition by Turner also provided opportunities for Hanna-Barbera properties to be incorporated into merchandise and entertainment vehicles throughout the Turner organization. Various Turner companies oversee the creation of interactive software, publishing, films, theme park attractions, and audio; Turner's Cartoon Network also offers opportunities for cooperation.

Three examples illustrate the cooperative process. First is the emphasis on Jonny Quest, cited earlier. The impetus for focusing on this character originated with Hanna-Barbera, which identified an interest in the marketplace in action properties in general and Jonny specifically. That led other Turner companies to see what they could do with the character in 1996. A second example is Space Ghost, who is also being considered for more licensing activity, not just within the "Hero Battalion" brand mentioned earlier but also in his own right. That possibility was engendered by the Cartoon Network, which developed an original program—*Space Ghost: Coast to Coast*, a live-action talk show in which the animated Space Ghost interacts with live guests—based on the classic character. Finally, a new concept, "Cave Kids," based on Pebbles and

Bamm-Bamm of *The Flintstones*, was generated by Turner Licensing & Merchandising. Responding to demand from retailers for an infant-oriented brand, Turner developed appropriate designs and is lining up licensees. In turn, other arms of the company are researching whether the concept is appropriate for television, publishing, home video, and so on.

In contrast to the studio's outlook in the 1960s and 1970s, licensing is currently regarded as an important facet of Hanna-Barbera's marketing plans (as it is throughout Turner Broadcasting System). The production of new entertainment vehicles is still the studio's core focus, and not every new or classic property within the library is considered merchandisable. Licensing royalties are no longer looked upon as ancillary, however, but are viewed as a major source of revenue. The appearance of licensed merchandise at retail is also perceived as an important element in revitalizing a classic property.

Star Trek

The *Star Trek* licensing program illustrates the power of new entertainment vehicles to rejuvenate and then keep a long-term property fresh over time. It is also notable for having a dual market consisting of a strong adult fan base that views the property as a classic, in addition to younger consumers for whom the program is new.

Building a franchise

Licensed merchandise based on the *Star Trek* franchise has far surpassed the $1 billion mark at retail, according to licensor Viacom Consumer Products. The vast majority of those sales have occurred since 1990, which marked the fourth season of original *Star Trek: The Next Generation* episodes and the first year that reruns of *TNG* were available in strip form. In fact, more than 200 licensees worldwide, in both upstairs and downstairs distribution tiers, accounted for $500 million in sales in 1994.

The original *Star Trek*, starring William Shatner as Captain James T. Kirk, debuted in 1966. Seventy-nine episodes were created, which are currently syndicated in 94% of the country (in more than 100 markets). Very little licensing activity for that series occurred until recently, with current licensees for the original show now including Franklin Mint for collectibles, Pocket Books, Interplay Productions for software, and Hamilton Gifts.

A large licensing program was developed for the first *Star Trek* movie in 1979, which starred the cast of the original series, but sell-in to retailers was low and the program did not meet expectations. A change of management in the Viacom Consumer Products (then Paramount Pictures) licensing department and the launch of *TNG* in 1987 led to a renewed licensing effort. Prior to 1990, however, the program focused primarily on adult-oriented items; a toy line that was in place during *TNG's* first few years did not generate significant sales.

In 1990, the stripped *TNG* reruns caused children to get to know the characters, and led to the signing of master toy licensee Playmates. Deals followed for home products and housewares, apparel, and packaged goods, among other categories.

Entertainment vehicles

One of the factors behind the current strength of the *Star Trek* licensing program is the awareness generated by the many entertainment and other media vehicles based on it. In addition to the original series, syndicated in seventy-five countries, and *TNG*, reruns of which are still widely syndicated (although 1993/94 was its last year in first-run syndication), there are two other television series: *Star Trek: Deep Space Nine* (Figure 5.7), which debuted in 1992 and as of this writing airs in more than 140 markets, and *Star Trek: Voyager*, which was launched in January 1995 as the anchor of the new United/Paramount network. Viacom estimates that a *Star Trek* program is on the air twice a day in virtually every television market.

As for motion pictures, six films starring the original cast have generated a total of nearly $500 million in box-office take, and all are available on home video (as are many of the television episodes). A seventh film, *Star Trek Generations* (the first starring the cast of *TNG*), was released in fall 1994, with another expected to be released approximately every two years. Although each entertainment vehicle has a separate merchandising program with its own list of licensees, more than 50% of the manufacturers have rights to all four television shows. This situation minimizes competition (e.g., *Voyager* licensees do not compete with *Deep Space Nine*

FIGURE 5.7   A set from *Star Trek: Deep Space Nine*. Spin-off series keep the *Star Trek* franchise fresh, introduce it to new audiences, and provide opportunities for promotions.
© 1994 Paramount Pictures. All Rights Reserved. Photo Credit: Robbie Robinson.

licensees), thus avoiding confusion and oversaturation in the marketplace.

Other entertainment/media ventures also add to the total number of impressions generated by the property. A vast publishing program is one example. More than 63 million *Star Trek* books are in print in fifteen languages, with a new *Star Trek* novel published every month; thirty classic *Star Trek* novels have appeared on the *New York Times* best-seller list since 1986. The *Star Trek Encyclopedia*, which was released in May 1994, has more than 200,000 copies in print, and a series of books on tape, narrated by actors from *Star Trek* and *TNG*, is also available.

Consumer electronics is a large product category (about 15% of the total) and also a means of generating further consumer impressions for the property. Interactive games and computer software for various platforms are available from licensees such as Paramount Interactive (a sister company of Viacom Consumer Products), Spectrum HoloByte, and Sega, among others, while Berkeley Systems makes screen savers and Bitstream markets type fonts.

A dual audience

Like other classic properties that have been around long enough to be known to two generations, the *Star Trek* franchise appeals to a dual audience of children and adults. As noted, the interest of today's children began to blossom in 1990 as they got to know the characters in *TNG*. After that interest became evident, master toy licensee Playmates was signed, generating $100 million in retail sales in 1993, its first year on the market, with more than 100 products, including action figures, accessories, and role-playing games. Playmates subsequently signed to produce toys based on all four television shows.

Overall, purchasers of licensed products are approximately 60% adults and 40% children. This breakdown varies from category to category. The toys appeal primarily to children but also attract a significant market of adult collectors, while electronics and gifts are targeted mainly toward adults. Publishing is also primarily purchased by an adult audience, although the age group is being brought down with the publication of a young adult book series for early teens by licensee (and Paramount Pictures' and Viacom Consumer Products' sister company) Simon & Schuster.

The product mix

Key product categories for the *Star Trek* franchise include those that further audience awareness of the property, as noted above, such as publishing and consumer electronics (which accounted for more than $70 million in retail sales in 1993). Electronics also make sense in that they fit so well with the futuristic and technology-related themes of the property itself. In fact, Viacom tries to be aggressive in encouraging licensees to incorporate new technologies into products, although that can sometimes drive prices up.

As noted earlier, toys are a significant category. Gifts are also important, particularly for adult fans. Hallmark, for example, has sold out of its *Star Trek* keepsake ornament for the last four years, and for the last two years has supported the line with *Star Trek*–themed television advertising featuring actors from the shows.

Overall, the *Star Trek* product mix is rather unusual, with relatively few sales in certain product categories, such as apparel, that typically account for a large proportion of licensed sales, especially for properties with significant adult audiences. In fact, just 13% of sales are attributable to products outside of toys, electronics, gifts and collectibles, stationery, and publishing. Viacom strives to maintain the longevity of the program, says management, by avoiding the tendency to overlicense the property, and by trying to stick with categories and products that make sense.

Viacom Consumer Products views licensing as an important part of the overall revenue/profit picture for *Star Trek*. In addition, despite the fact that the franchise is so well established, licensing also helps create awareness, in particular for newly launched television shows and films.

Chapter 6

The Future of Television Merchandising

Changes in Licensing and Television Businesses Continue

Many of the trends outlined in this book should continue to develop as the future unfolds. The increasingly conservative outlook on the part of manufacturers and especially retailers toward entertainment licensing, which began during the recession of the early 1990s but remains as the economy pulls out of its doldrums, should continue. Retailers seem to limit their demand to classic properties supplemented by one or two hot properties a year. This situation may change somewhat from season to season, depending on what licenses are available, but the overriding trend should continue. This means that "B" properties—fairly strong, but neither classic nor blockbuster—may face a difficult time. More opportunities will develop for niche programs, but "B" properties that licensors hope will become widely merchandised may face difficult barriers. In television licensing, children's animation will be most affected.

The more a licensor—especially the owner of a new television show, which is perceived as particularly risky due to the threat of quick cancellation—can do to convince licensees and retailers of the property's potential longevity, the better the chance that manufacturers will be drawn to the property, and that they will be able to sell to retailers. After all, there are a lot of properties out there from which to choose. Strong support by the licensor in terms of promotions, entertainment spin-offs, and media ventures will continue to become more and more attractive to licensees and retailers alike.

Retailer conservatism drives another trend emphasized in this book, which is the propensity to look at any entertainment-driven property as just that, an *entertainment* property, as opposed to a television property or a film property. A property may originate as a television show, a film, a video game, a comic book, a toy, or a book character, or even spring from a direct-to-home-video release. But, increasingly, that property, no matter where it originates, will cross over into all of those areas and others as part of the quest to maximize its longevity and provide sales opportunities in as many windows as possible. Television is just part of the equation.

While this development will lead to greater sales of licensed merchandise overall and to increased awareness of a given property over the long term, it also means that more participants are involved in licensing. More players will cause revenues to be fragmented, while more decision-makers will be involved in all aspects of the merchandising program. A licensor should be aware of the potential challenges inherent in creating a multi-entertainment franchise from a television show, as well as recognizing the potential benefits of such a strategy.

As these changes persist, the importance of "fit"—between licensee and licensor, property and product, television viewership and retail consumer—cannot be overemphasized. Within the increasingly competitive atmosphere of entertainment licensing, successful product lines need to make sense. This advice has always applied to licensing, of course, but it becomes crucial as retailers and consumers become more savvy about entertainment-related merchandise. Part of the appeal of licensed products based on television shows or other entertainment has always been their novelty. They are different, and they are fun. Increasingly, however, entertainment products as a group are not unusual; they have been around for more than fifteen years in a big way. Still, if the application of the license to a given product is appropriate, that item may indeed have an element of uniqueness, and as such may be fun to purchase and own.

The maturation of the licensing business means that companies who are active in it will continue to become more sophisticated and creative in the ways they utilize the tools and techniques of merchandising. At the same time, a steady stream of television companies new to licensing will enter the field, as the ever-increasing number of television distribution channels leads to progressively more programming, resulting in a greater number of potentially licensable properties.

These new players will seek to take advantage of the ability of licensing to create awareness of their shows and brands and to generate funding for their production efforts. And, while the search for the "next Barney" or the "next Power Rangers" won't cease any time soon, more television licensors will become aware that merchandising offers several possible marketing options aside from generating retail sales of $1 billion in a short period of time. Niche properties and smaller, even offbeat, licensing efforts will be increasingly attractive and viable. Each of these properties may have fewer licensing partners, but the chance of success for individual licensees still exists.

Completely new licensed products should continue to develop as accepted categories—such as headwear (caps) and trading cards—become saturated and as manufacturers in untapped categories see the potential of licensing. Technological advances and an increased emphasis on creativity should also drive this trend. For example, in the mid-1990s, some previously unheard-of product categories have quickly blossomed, such as milk caps (trading card–like collectible games), prepaid phone cards, and computer screensavers. Some of these categories are faddish and will wane after a brief time, while others will be longer lasting. In either case, this changing environment will mean continuous new opportunities for licensors, licensees, and retailers, and should keep a property's existing customers' interest piqued, while attracting new customers who have never bought licensed merchandise in the past.

People frequently wonder if licensing will lose its popularity or if sales of licensed merchandise have peaked. Licensing is not a fad. It is an accepted marketing technique, and will continue to be so. Why? Consumers do not buy licensed merchandise because they have an inherent love for licensing. They purchase licensed products because they like the property and, more specifically, because they like the way that property is applied to a given item. The purchaser of Barney merchandise is not the same as the purchaser of *Seinfeld* products. At the same time, there is no law that says a person who is a devotee of *The Andy Griffith Show* merchandise cannot buy *I Love Lucy* items as well. Consumer whims dictate that a given property may come and go, but licensing, as an effective marketing tool, is here to stay.

Interactivity and Multimedia

The development of viable interactive television technologies and multimedia products—possibly incorporating household television sets as well as audio, computers, and musical equipment—is widely viewed throughout the television and licensing businesses as virtually certain. Exactly what format these technologies will take is as yet unknown, however. It is unclear which technologies will develop first into marketable entities, and it is also debatable which, if any, current technologies will capture consumers' imaginations. The future of interactive multimedia is dependent not only upon technological advances but also upon demand from consumers as they cast their votes in the marketplace.

No matter which interactive technologies ultimately survive, however, a number of relevant considerations for television licensors will arise. On the positive side, an increasing number of interactive applications will lead to more potential product categories in which to license television-based properties. This is already beginning to occur. For example, five years ago, the installed base of home computers was minuscule compared to what it is today. As more consumers began to purchase personal computers for home rather than business use, however, a large enough market developed for computer-related merchandise to become attractive to licensors. At the same time, the number of manufacturers offering home-computer-related products grew, meaning that there were more potential licensees from which licensors could choose. In addition, these manufacturers sought out licenses to differentiate themselves in the face of increasing competition. Thus new licensed product categories sprang up, ranging from software applications and utilities—screensavers, type fonts, sound effects, and animated icons—to computer accessories such as mouse pads, screen frames, and mouse covers.

A parallel situation has occurred within the video-game industry. As available platforms proliferate, television licensors are able to authorize their properties for an increasing number of game formats. In the early 1990s, Sega and Nintendo were the dominant forces, and 16-bit games were just being introduced. As of this writing, however, existing platforms include 8-bit (those that still remain), 16-bit, 32-bit, 64-bit, and CD-based games, and hardware is available from (or being developed by) not only Sega and Nintendo, but 3DO, Atari, Sony, Philips, and others. A similar situation has occurred with computer-based multimedia platforms as well, with no standard platform emerging as a clear leader. This proliferation of formats should continue with the advent of further technological breakthroughs.

Concurrent with their rising importance as licensed products, multimedia and interactive technologies will—because of their growing installed base and their mounting influence on popular culture worldwide—be a deepening source of licensed properties. Five or so years ago, video and computer games were thought of primarily as destinations for licensed properties. As of this writing, however, a large number of properties available for licensing originate as characters in electronic games. They then often move on to become films or television shows in their own right. In addition to the video-game characters enumerated in Chapter 3, examples extend to CD-ROM properties, such as Id Software's Doom and Cyan's Myst.

While the number of new platforms and technologies is a financial boon to television licensors since there are more opportunities for incoming royalty streams, this proliferation also worsens the competitive situation discussed earlier. Producers of traditional television shows will not only face competition from the plethora of broadcast, cable, pay-per-view, and satellite-delivered programming, but will also compete for audience share—and for licensees and licensed product consumers—with interactive programming, be it television-based, such as the Sega Channel, or in another format, such as CD-ROM.

Companies in the television and licensing businesses want to position themselves to be able to capitalize on whatever happens in the future, so that they can compete, or at least survive. Yet they are not certain what actions to take now, because they lack knowledge about exactly what the future will bring. They strive to strike a balance. On the one hand, they want to adequately invest in new technologies—whether through licensing, joint ventures, in-house divisions, or subsidiaries—to be poised for the future. On the other hand, they hope to minimize their investment in technologies that ultimately do not pan out.

Rights

Another ramification of both interactivity and multimedia—whether or not the two attributes are combined into a single technology—is the increasing complexity of the division of rights. First of all, the new technologies require massive amounts of content. This information, when not original, is obtained from various rights holders, such as publishers, artists, photographers, actors, musicians, and trademark licensors. Assembling such products can be a long nightmare of rights clearances. It is often uncertain, for example, who owns the rights to a given property, especially if the property was created prior to the development of today's technology. Even home video did not exist, much less other more advanced technologies, when many film and television properties were launched.

Second, spin-off properties are often created within the context of multimedia or interactive products. That is, new properties—such as characters, plot lines, designs, or environments—originate during the creation of software for the new medium. Ownership of copyrights, patents, and trademarks of these new properties must be decided, whether they are divided among the original property owner or owners and whoever developed the new creation, or allocated to one of the parties.

Third, the fact that true interactivity implies the ability of the end user to manipulate the software—and the licensed properties therein—gives rise to some approval problems. For example, the end user of an interactive product could theoretically cause Bugs Bunny to swear, make Betty Boop wear lewd or no clothing, or cause Spiderman to interact with a Playboy Bunny. Many of these interactions and newly created language or looks may not be desirable to the property owner, to say the least. To prevent such situations, licensors are likely to want restrictions placed on how their characters can be used within the context of the software. These restraints limit the amount of true interactivity that can occur. This dichotomy between the image a rights holder wants to maintain for its property and the attributes that a software developer requires for true interactivity and technological superiority promises to become greater as capabilities become more sophisticated.

Because technologies are leapfrogging each other at such a fast pace, many rights-related problems are still developing. The body of law governing multimedia and interactive rights is playing catch-up. Copyright and trademark laws, as originally written, do not deal specifically with interactive multimedia creations, and, so far, few legal precedents exist for such disputes. Until a body of precedents is developed, the court system must rely on parallel cases such as those that arose when home video was created, causing similar types of disputes.

At the same time, out-of-date publishing and entertainment contracts do not deal with rights to technologies that could not have been imagined when the agreements were forged. New entertainment-related agreements do, however, take into account the fact that currently unimagined technologies will be created, and incorporate contractual wording with that in mind.

Transactional Television

The number of transactional television outlets should continue to rise. Transactional television—television programming that combines entertainment and merchandise sales—includes home shopping networks, syndicated or cable transactional television series, one-minute spots during which merchandise is sold, and infomercials. These venues have proven to be effective ways of moving certain types of merchandise, particularly housewares, home exercise equipment, and health and beauty products. As manufacturers look for nontraditional ways to sell their products, and as retailers become aware that home shopping tends to drive traditional retail sales rather than cannibalize them, more and more transactional television opportunities should become available.

As far as licensing is concerned, this development will affect television companies in two major ways. First, transactional programming offers new outlets for licensed merchandise based on television shows. Finding new ways to sell merchandise is attractive to both licensees and licensors, particularly as retail consolidation and other factors lead to conservative purchasing decisions by retailers. Many licensors and individual licensees are testing various types of transactional television programming, in many cases with success.

The list of television-based licensors who have experimented with selling products over the airwaves is growing. Viacom Consumer Products with *Star Trek*, All American with *Baywatch*, MCA / Universal with *Northern Exposure* and *Coach*, and Fox with *The Simpsons* have all experimented with selling merchandise through short-form commercials.

Television-related licensors who have gathered merchandise from their licensees for segments on home shopping network QVC include ABC Daytime with *All My Children*, Viacom with *Star Trek*, Saban with *Mighty Morphin Power Rangers*, and United Media with *Peanuts*. Products are often exclusive to the transactional venue, but manufactured by existing retail licensees; a one- or two-hour segment can generate total retail sales in the hundreds of thousands of dollars.

Licensors currently view transactional television as being in a test phase. A number of details are still being worked out, including the financial structure of the deals, how much product exclusivity is necessary, and which product categories sell best. Yet most feel that home shopping has potential, at least for generating awareness for their properties, if not for great quantities of purchases.

In addition to providing opportunities for sales of licensed merchandise, transactional shows also offer the potential for producers and networks to create ancillary revenue streams through sales of licensed merchandise, whether based on their own programming or on other properties. For example, MTV, ESPN, and Nickelodeon are all experimenting with transactional programming, during which licensed products and other merchandise is sold on air. Retail sales of approximately $1 million in licensed Woodstock merchandise was sold on MTV during its coverage of Woodstock '94, for example, while ESPN ran about a dozen shows in 1994 (with more planned for 1995) called *NASCAR Shop Talk*, featuring licensed auto racing merchandise. Nickelodeon has created exclusive on-air product promotions based on its Nick at Nite lineup and plans further home shopping tests.

Increasingly Global Nature of Television and Licensing

Both the licensing business and the television industry are becoming increasingly global. In terms of merchandising, U.S. licensors expect international markets to exhibit faster growth rates in the coming years than the domestic market. Of the $97.8 billion in worldwide sales of licensed merchandise in 1993, more than two-thirds was sold in the United States and Canada, according to *The Licensing Letter.* Of the remaining one-third, a bit less than two-thirds is attributable to Europe and a bit less than one-third to Japan. Australia/New Zealand is a strong market in per-capita purchases of licensed merchandise, but is small in total population, and the remainder of the world market for licensed products is in its infancy.

At the same time that U.S. licensors are looking outward for opportunities, international licensors are also increasing their merchandising activity, both in their own territories and internationally. Although the vast majority (about 85%, according to *The Licensing Letter*) of total sales of licensed merchandise worldwide are attributable to properties originating in the United States, a growing number of licenses from outside North America are available domestically. Some of the international properties that have a presence in the United States include the British Broadcasting Corporation's Mr. Blobby; Tintin, an Ellipse Programme/Nelvana co-production in association with Fondation Hergé, based on a French-language comic book and currently airing on Nickelodeon; author Beatrix Potter's characters, airing in a series on HBO in the United States; *Sailor Moon*, a Japanese program being launched in the United States in syndication in 1995; and *Johnson & Friends*, from Film Australia in association with WQED-TV, which is on the Fox Network in the United States. In fact, several international licensors and licensing agents are specifically targeting the U.S. market, opening offices to better serve what they consider a growth area for their properties.

At the same time, international television companies are becoming more active in the licensing business. Many organizations, including the British Broadcasting Corporation, are setting up licensing subsidiaries to merchandise properties that gain exposure on their networks, including those that they produce in-house. In addition, networks are increasingly looking to include licensing as part of their distribution deals. They want a percentage of merchandising revenues in return for the exposure they give a show by airing it in their territory.

International distribution is becoming increasingly important to the total profit picture for television productions (Figure 6.1). As a result, the average lead time between when a program is broadcast in the United States or its country of origination and when it is launched internationally is decreasing. In fact, some programs are introduced worldwide or in several territories at a time, nearly simultaneously, although generally there is still a lag of about a year between the U.S. launch of a show and its international rollout.

In terms of licensing, this shortening of lead times means that merchandising programs must increasingly be planned on a worldwide basis up front. Worldwide launches of licensing programs are

FIGURE 6.1 *Space Precinct*, distributed by Grove Television Enterprises, is one of many examples of television programs with international distribution and multi-territory licensing plans.

© 1994 The Space Precinct Limited Partnership.

even possible and will probably increase as lead times get shorter and the number of international co-productions rises. Such simultaneous worldwide launch strategies promise to be riskier for international licensees. Currently, when a program is sold to licensees abroad it has a track record in the United States. Despite cultural differences, a program that has demonstrated success in the United States is more likely to be successful abroad. In addition, a licensing program that has failed to meet expectations in the United States can be fine-tuned before the show is introduced worldwide, and can still be a success there despite its U.S. track record. A simultaneous worldwide launch means that all territories will face the same risks as the initial countries face, and that selling the property to licensees and consumers internationally will be more difficult.

As television companies look for more creative ways to finance their productions in the face of rising costs, more global ventures occur, drawing resources from entities around the world. For example, the series *The Animals of Farthing Wood*, handled for licensing by the BBC, has sixteen European co-production partners. Such arrangements increase the chances even further that more global, or at least multi-territorial, licensing efforts will be implemented, some being launched nearly simultaneously across borders. Producers and/or financiers in various territories, as they seek ways to recoup their investments, will increasingly recognize royalties from sales of licensed merchandise as one method of doing so.

As agreements among the parties involved in a show's creation and production become more complicated, the division of rights and responsibilities—copyright and trademark ownership, licensing revenues, day-to-day licensing program administration, and product approvals—becomes more tangled as well. Good relationships, mutual understanding, and parallel objectives—among partners, as well as between licensees and licensors—will become even more important in complicated multi-territory arrangements than they already are in a typical domestic deal.

In addition to the increasingly international nature of the agreements behind individual productions, television-related brands, particularly cable channels, are also being launched worldwide. For example, CNN, MTV, Nickelodeon, and other cable networks are expanding globally, and their licensing efforts target consumers worldwide as well. The U.S. broadcast networks are also developing an increased branded presence abroad, particularly due to the spread of U.S. news organizations. U.S. entertainment programming has been known around the world for years, and now its news personalities and network brands are beginning to be recognized, too.

While the approach to licensing varies from territory to territory, the creation of worldwide television brands will contribute to the increasingly global licensing business. It will hasten the spread of U.S. pop culture—much of which finds its form in licensed merchandise—and the territorial differences between regions should gradually lessen. Still, when embarking on a worldwide licensing program it should be remembered that cultures, tastes, political and economic climates, and retail infrastructures vary from territory to territory. It will be a very long time before one licensing program can truly cover the whole world without variations from region to region in strategy, products, and even character attributes.

Television Licensing in the Face of Uncertainty

It is one thing to try to predict the future and quite another to know exactly what actions to take now in order to be best positioned for the coming years. It is fairly safe to say that "interactivity" of some sort will increase over the next decade, for example, but it is virtually impossible to predict just how. And, while most companies in both the television and licensing businesses know that it is important to adapt to the changing environment, it is difficult to know what specific steps to take.

Licensors agree, however, that flexibility is one prerequisite. An organization that is able to anticipate and stay one step ahead of changes, or even to quickly react to new developments, will be likely to prosper.

APPENDIX I

Licensing Periodicals

The Licensing Letter, EPM Communications, Brooklyn, NY

The Licensing Book, New York, NY

The Licensing Journal, Grimes & Battersby, New York, NY

Index, Fairchild Publications, New York, NY

Licensing Trends, Geyer-McAllister Publications, New York, NY

Licensing Reporter Europe, A4 Publications, Stourbridge, UK

APPENDIX II

Licensing Resource Books

EPM Licensing Letter Sourcebook, EPM Communications, Brooklyn, NY

The Licensing Business Handbook, EPM Communications, Brooklyn, NY

The International Licensing Directory, A4 Publications, Stourbridge, UK

The Guide to the Licensing World, Cascade Publishing, Nutley, UK

The Licensing Resource Directory, Expocon, Fairfield, CT

A Primer on Licensing, Kent Press, Stamford, CT

APPENDIX III

Trade Association and Trade Shows

Association

International Licensing Industry Merchandiser's Association (LIMA), New York, NY

Trade Shows

Licensing '95 Exposition and Conference, held in June in New York, sponsored by LIMA, New York, NY

The Worldwide Licensing Exposition, held in April in London, sponsored by *The Licensing Book*, New York, NY

EPM Entertainment Marketing Conference, held in November in Los Angeles, sponsored by EPM Communications, Brooklyn, NY

Index